"Angie Smith has the rare gift to write a non-fiction page turner as good as any fiction book I've read. As her words tumbled out in raw honesty, fresh hope spread before me. Her teachings on fear are comforting, practical, and gut honest. I can't wait for you to read this life-changing book. *What Women Fear* is one of my favorites this year. Honestly, I think it will stay next to my bed for a very long time."

—Lysa TerKeurst, *New York Times* best-selling author of fourteen books including, *Made to Crave*

"You don't have to be around Angie Smith very long to fall in love with her. She is funny and transparent with a passionate love for Christ. In *What Women Fear* Angie holds up a mirror so that we can see ourselves from every angle, the thoughts we display on the front shelves of our lives and those we hide. The greatest gift tucked into this book is the overwhelming picture of the mercy of our God who understands our fears and invites us to stand beside Him in the rain and let His love wash us clean."

—Sheila Walsh, author of *The Shelter of God's Promises*

"Whatever high wire you're walking right now, there really is nobody you want at the other end of the line like Angie Smith. And this rare gem of a book is like a steadying, sure hand—taking you right into His presence in ways you never imagined. Vivid, profoundly biblical, yet girlfriend real with just-the-medicine-you-need-funny, every page is reviving hope for every woman. Simply, Angie Smith is a Bible teacher for such a time as this."

—Ann Voskamp, *New York Times* best-selling author of *One Thousand Gifts*

WHAT WOMEN FEAR

WALKING *in* FAITH *that* TRANSFORMS

WHAT
WOMEN
FEAR

WALKING *in* FAITH *that* TRANSFORMS

ANGIE SMITH

NASHVILLE, TENNESSEE

978-0-8054-6429-0

Published by B&H Publishing Group
Nashville, Tennessee

Dewey Decimal Classification: 248.843
Subject Heading: FEAR \ WOMEN \ FAITH

1 2 3 4 5 6 7 8 • 15 14 13 12 11

For my father,

*the man who made it easy to believe
I could trust my Father.*

CONTENTS

DID HE REALLY SAY THAT?

THE QUESTION THAT STARTED THE QUESTIONS

I have long been fascinated by the questions God asks in Scripture. It's obvious He knows the answers, so why does He ask? We see this throughout the Old Testament as well as the New, and it is such a beautiful image of the way Christ loves us. He gives opportunity after opportunity for us to share what's on our hearts with Him.

As I read, I noticed that many times He responded to someone who appeared to be struggling with fear by asking a question of them. And I also noticed that at first glance they seemed like kind of strange questions. I mean, the disciples are clinging to life in a boat that's being thrown around the ocean and the best He can do is ask them where their faith is? Seriously? Or when He's wrestling Jacob, who is fearful about facing off with his brother the next day, and God asks him what his name is. Doesn't He know his name? I mean, He's God, right?

Of course He knows Jacob's name, just like He knows yours and mine. What He wants from this interaction is a confession of sorts; an acknowledgment of who Jacob is in his own eyes.

Scripture repeatedly shows us how God uses questions to reveal something about the heart of the person He is speaking to. Each question was for their benefit so they could be aware of a lesson He was teaching them. There is accountability and forced recognition of the words we have in response to these questions, and I believe there is great wisdom to be gained by considering them.

Interestingly, the very first question posed in the Bible is not spoken by God, but rather by Satan himself disguised as a snake. It is a simple, profound sentence that changes everything.

We learn that Satan doesn't have to force us to do anything sinful; he merely needs to plant a seed of doubt and let us tangle ourselves up in it. What he does in the Garden of Eden is introduce a concept that haunts each and every one of us every day of our lives.

Adam and Eve have been told not to eat fruit from one particular tree and they don't seem to be too concerned about that prohibition until the snake makes a casual comment.

"Did God *really say,* 'You must not eat from any tree in the garden'?" (Genesis 3:1, italics mine).

Did He? Because I'm wondering if you're sure you heard Him right. Maybe there's a little room for negotiation, Eve. I mean, it could have been a misunderstanding, right?

Eve responds by saying, "We may eat of the fruit of the trees in the garden, but God said, 'You shall not eat of the fruit of the tree that is in the midst of the garden, neither shall you touch it, lest you die'" (Genesis 3:2–3 ESV).

Reading this makes me think of my daughter Ellie, who is a strict rule-keeper. What makes me smile in both instances is the immediate desire to defend the rules. It's entirely possible that God told Eve not to touch the tree, but we don't see that anywhere in Scripture. He tells her not to *eat* from it, but He never says anything about *touching* it. Maybe like my Ellie she had put up a little extra protection in her mind so she wouldn't break the eating rule.

But, in the event that she thought she had misunderstood . . . now *that* would be different . . .

Satan doesn't miss a beat. He has planted the seed of doubt in her mind and then he goes in for the kill.

Okay, so you want to keep the rules. Fine. But do you know why He doesn't want you to eat? Because you could be wise like He is, and He doesn't want that. You won't die, you'll just be a little more like God.

Well, that does it. Eve grabs herself some fruit and then offers a bit to her husband.

I like to imagine the conversation that happened before the fig leaves were added to wardrobe.

"Eve! What are you thinking? God told us we can't eat that stuff!"

"Adam, it's *fiiiiiine*. I just met the nicest talking snake and he assured me there was a little confusion about that. We aren't going to die, we're going to get wiser!"

Adam sure doesn't stick up for the old rulebook. He dives right in without any apparent rebuttal, and immediately everything changes—not just for them, but for all of us.

Never once did Satan tell her to eat the fruit; all he did was ask her if she was sure.

And then I think she wondered if God really had her best interest in mind.

We aren't so different, are we?

At this point, sin enters the world, and fear comes right along with it. As Adam and Eve sew up their new loincloths, they know they have made a mistake and that they are going to be in trouble.

They act out of fear, and so do we. We do it in all kinds of ways, and while it's different for each person, the heart of it is the same. We are responding to the lie of Satan each and every time we run. Fundamentally, every single fear comes from the lie spoken by the enemy in a garden designed to be a haven: *Are you sure? Are you really, really sure? Because you are staking your life on a claim that you might have just misunderstood. God says He is good . . . is He? He tells you He has your best in mind . . . does He? He boasts that He is almighty, all-knowing, all together trustworthy . . . is He?*

What a powerful way to get us to fall into the trap. He doesn't quite push us in, but he doesn't have to. We do a pretty good job of jumping once the doubt is there. For the remainder of this book, I want to encourage you to change your thinking about fear. Instead of it being a black and white, you do or you don't, you succeed or you fail kind of issue, I want to propose that it is more of a balancing act than anything else. I don't think I'm a failure because I have had fears, and I certainly don't think that it is a requirement for Christians to forego fear in order to be good followers of Christ. I believe fear is the natural response to the question Satan whispered, and I find that every day I have to adjust my footing consciously to move toward Jesus.

In my mind's eye I see a woman teetering on a tightrope, holding a long pole as she tries to balance herself in light of the truth of God. It takes concentration, it takes work, and it takes a whole lot of faith. Some of us are currently tipped so far in the wrong direction that we don't know if we will be able to right ourselves, and others are walking with arms outstretched while their feet confidently move one in front of the other. As life goes on, we will probably experience both, and what we will find is that it is always changing. Situations come up and cause us to tip a little, and we cry out in fear. We often feel like just as we get it figured out, the wire begins to shake and we have to adjust it all over again.

We (mistakenly) believe that at some point we are going to find the solution, learn how to balance the pole exactly right in every moment so that we don't ever tremble anymore. We think we can overcome it so that it never rears its head again, and that the rest of our days will be smooth sailing. I don't believe there is such a thing, and the more we focus our attention on the rope, the less we focus on the pole in our hands. It isn't like there is one solution that will erase all our fears, one way to do it, one single thing that will take it away and make it simple. That's not how God designed us.

I have heard it said that God is like the net in this example; that He will catch us if we fall, that He is our safe place, that we need not fear because we always have that waiting if things get bad enough. I don't disagree, but I think that many of us have put our emphasis on the net rather than the pole in our hands. We have access to Him here, in the moment, in every situation that arises. The more we tap into a life balanced by Christ, grounded in knowing Him and His Word, the less we have to worry about falling off. It's still scary up here, no question, but if we can get a firm grip on that which steadies us, it will look different.

Have you been living life with Jesus as the net? I know for many seasons of life, I have. He's there if I really need Him, but at this moment I just need to figure out how to get myself straightened and keep moving.

Balance. I think it's more about that than anything else. What are we depending on when we start to tip? How do we develop the kind of thinking that steadies us? Why do we react the way we do when the rope shakes and the wind comes from nowhere? We all want to live lives that rely on the power of Christ, but we don't necessarily know how to get to the point where we are doing that. My prayer is that as we work through some of the major categories of fear and dig deep into our own experiences, we will see that there are patterns in our thinking that have thrown us off balance. As I read through Scripture I was so blessed by studying the questions God asks in His Word, and doubly blessed at the responses of His servants. Daily now, I hear those questions at the heart of my fears, and before I am tempted to believe I am never going to take another step, I answer them in my heart and with my actions. I am better prepared when life comes at me and I rely on armor I never turned to before.

What did they fear? What did He ask? How did they answer? *How do we?*

Let's dig in with God's question to Adam and Eve, shall we? Okay, back to the garden we go . . .

Genesis tells us that they heard the sound of the Lord God walking in the garden and they immediately hid. Here's where God's first recorded question occurs.

"Where are you?" He called out.

In the event that you're curious, God knew where they were. Although it would have certainly been noteworthy if He were really asking for the sake of determining their location, like He had lost the first two people He ever made. *Oh well, back to the drawing board. Maybe next time . . .*

Although we can never truly know the mind and motives of God, I suspect that He asked the question because He wanted Adam and Eve to tell Him the answer, and in doing so, confess their transgression. He wasn't asking them to identify their location, but rather their *condition*. And maybe also to teach them that cowering behind trees doesn't really do that much good when you're hiding from the God of the universe. Just a thought.

Adam responded, "I heard the sound of you in the garden and I was afraid, because I was naked, and I hid myself" (Genesis 3:10 ESV).

Where are you?

I was afraid, Lord. So I hid . . .

════════════

Santa was coming.

I knew it was true because the news had done a special weather update and it showed a fuzzy radar picture of his sleigh traveling around the world. My parents popped popcorn on the stove and we were glued to the TV. We had been counting down the days with a little tabletop calendar, and we were finally there. This was it.

I was fascinated by him.

Who could do that? The whole traveling thing wasn't nearly as interesting to me as the fact that he knew who was naughty. I mean, it was certainly logistically complicated to do all that in one night, and if weather patterns didn't cooperate or if the reindeer got antsy, well, there could be trouble.

Logically, yes. It could be complicated.

But who in the world knows every single move a kid makes and then decides whether or not they're going to get candy? Now that is some serious pressure.

Who has time for "Jingle Bells"? Who cares about chestnuts and where they're roasting? There were much more important things at stake. There was only one Christmas song I memorized as a four-year-old; the one it all boiled down to in the end.

"He's making a list, he's checkin' it twice. Gonna find out who's naughty and nice . . ."

Oh wow.

He's checking it *twice.*

Nothing gets by this guy.

My little sister arranged the cookies on the plate, taking a bite of each as she went. She had icing all over her face, so it was probably futile at this point, but in the event that the big guy was still making adjustments to his list, I did what any good sister would do. I whacked her arm and pointed up at the chimney while opening my eyes wide to remind her he was watching.

She dropped the cookie and cried.

My parents told me to knock it off. Clearly they were not concerned about her stocking this year.

Oh well. I tried.

For weeks it had been like this.

My mom would tell me to get my clothes on and I would run to my closet, thinking *he's watching, he's watching . . . hurry!*

I ate everything on my plate, including things that were green. I didn't even dare play with my dolls because I might make a mess and forget to clean it up. I brushed my teeth like my life depended on my dental hygiene.

I was tormented by all the Christmas decorations and the stores showing pictures of him all decked out in his suit, like there was a taunting clock counting down to judgment day. Everyone was so casual about it. Didn't they know he was even watching them sleep? He knew when they were awake! I figured I better just be good for goodness sake.

He sure acted like a nice guy when I told him what I wanted. He looked just like the pictures and he "Ho, ho, ho'ed" and told me he was going to feed his reindeer.

I wasn't fooled. He knew how bad I was and he was going to make me pay.

I can just imagine myself in line, smoothing down my black

velvet dress and assessing my competition as I threw in some last-minute prayers.

I'm willing to bet I tried to get Santa's attention when the kids started roughhousing next to me.

But there was always that nagging voice that had already found a home in so many of my thoughts—*what if?* It all came down to this, and we were going to sing happy songs and dress pretty and then just hope we made the big cut. And I for one was not unaware of the consequences of my sin.

Christmas morning wasn't for those who disobeyed and blamed the dog "falling" down the stairs on her sister. No way that had gotten past him.

I smiled for the obligatory "Christmas nightgown and cookies" picture and then I hightailed it up to my bedroom. For the record, I still have this picture and I look like I'm drugged. Apparently fear did strange things to my face. The horrific bowl haircut (thank you, Mother) was totally unrelated but equally disturbing.

I hopped into bed and pulled the covers up to my neck. I stared at the two plastic candles my mom had taped down on the windowsill with masking tape. It was so quiet in my room, and I squeezed my eyes shut so I could focus on talking to him.

"Santa, I know you've been watching. And if you want to wake me up when you get here, I can explain about the dog thing." I cleared my throat and continued on explaining all the mistakes that came to mind.

It was my first attempt at confession. And naturally, it was to a fictitious man who flew reindeer. Welcome to my world.

"What if I haven't been good enough?" I whispered.

Tears started spilling down my cheeks and I rolled over in my bed and pulled the covers over me.

He can't see me in here, I thought. *I'm safe . . .*

And there, on December 24, 1980, I learned what it felt like to try and hide from the One Who was always watching.

Early in the morning, I heard my sister Jennifer rustling around. I could hear paper tearing and squeals coming from the family room.

I didn't budge. My nightgown was soaked through with sweat and I realized it was judgment time.

A few more minutes went by and I heard my door creak open. My dad came and sat next to me on the bed.

"Angela, your sister is already up and she's ripping through her presents. You want to join us?" He stroked my hair and smiled.

I burst into fresh tears, agonizing over what I should say. My dad still loved me, at least for the moment. But I had a feeling that might change when he saw the lump of coal waiting for me down the hall. Everyone was going to see it eventually so I might as well beat Santa to the punch and try for some Brownie points.

"Daddy, I'm a bad girl! He didn't bring me anything because I'm bad and he knows it! I'm not going out there, ever. EVER!!!!"

I started to pull the covers up again but my dad grabbed them from me.

"Honey, no! You're wrong! I've been in there and I saw what he brought and I really think you should go look. He brought you something you really wanted." He smiled expectantly and for a moment I was tempted to believe him.

I searched his eyes and considered the two quarters I had stolen from the money dish in the kitchen a few days prior.

Not a chance, pops.

"You're *LYING!!!!!* You're trying to trick me and I'm not going out there!!!!" This time I managed to fully disappear under the Holly Hobbie sheets. I was gasping for air now, terrified.

He stayed with me until I relented, but it wasn't without a fight. As I recall, he ended up carrying me to the family room while I stared over his shoulder instead of looking ahead. I made him tell me again that he saw toys for me when we got close, and when he assured me several more times I opened my eyes.

I will never forget the moment I looked for myself and saw that it was true. Santa had brought me pom-poms. The green and white pom-poms I wanted. This was monumental, not so much because it was what I was hoping for, but something much bigger than that. Something that would shape my thought process for the rest of my life.

He thought I was good enough. Maybe I don't need to be afraid of him anymore.

I danced around the house singing Christmas carols and jingling the bells on my Christmas sweater. Nothing could be better. I didn't care about the candy canes; I just wanted to be deemed *good.*

I didn't want to be in trouble with him, so I had hidden.

I might as well have chosen to cower under a couple trees.

To this day this is one of my parent's favorite stories to tell, and as I flip through photo albums and see the look on my face as I held the Barbie car in front of me for 300 million pictures, I can see the joy of a little girl whose innocence was intact and whose heart believed. But for me, part of the believing was fear.

He was checking it twice, after all.

When I think back to my childhood, there is so much joy and love. Despite this, there is a haunting feeling of fear I carried with me into adulthood. My parents did everything they could to help me, but to this day fear is a major part of my testimony. I won't say I feel qualified to tell you I have all the answers, nor will I promise that you will miraculously be cured of your anxiety by the time you reach the end of this book. What I will say is that I hope I am an encouraging companion to you as we go; a sister who understands your pain and the desire to live a life free of it. As I wrote this book I prayed for each person who would read it, asking God to make Himself known in a special way to those of you who are in bondage to fear.

I am also praying for those of you who are reading and wouldn't necessarily say you are fearful. I hope that some of the chapters will inspire you to be honest about parts of your life that you might not have put under the header of "fear." I truly believe that every single one of us struggles with some type of fear, whether it's fear of flying or fear of being "found out." Maybe you don't worry about dying but you get sick thinking about the fact that you might fail.

Throughout Scripture we have the opportunity to meet some amazing men and women whose stories remind us that we aren't alone, and that our fears and struggles are not unknown to God. I know that for good portions of this book I saw things I had never seen, and I believe the Lord opened my eyes to verses I had skimmed over many times, never fully grasping the magnitude of what was being offered.

I want you to hear my heart on this. I am not going to beat you over the head with a five-pound Bible and tell you that if you truly loved the Lord you would never fear. I don't think that's realistic. Yes, the Lord desires for you to be free from the bondage of fear, but it isn't reasonable to say you will never have fear again in your life if you are a good Christian. I have had people make me feel this way, probably without even knowing, and it hurt me deeply.

I have found so much comfort in the company of amazing men and women scattered from Genesis to Revelation who have given me hope that I don't have to do it alone. More than that, these people from the pages of the Bible have become friends to me over the years. I look to them for advice on how other people have dealt with true, human emotions. Some of them failed miserably. Honestly, that kind of takes the pressure off feeling like I might be the first one to simultaneously love God and feel like I'm disappointing Him.

Several years ago I was in a Bible study of amazing women; each and every one was someone I respected and trusted. One night a woman in study shared that she was terrified that something bad was going to happen to her. She started crying as she told us about horrific images that had tormented her. As she spoke I noticed that almost every single person was offering their version of what she had just said. Here we had been meeting for years and this had never come up. It was like the floodgates opened as a group of women sat side by side and shared things they had carried for decades because they thought nobody would understand. As I recall, there was only one girl who didn't say anything, and I'm pretty sure that was because she feared public speaking.

We have a very real enemy who thrives on our silence.

He doesn't want us to be in fellowship, sharing our hearts and seeking wisdom on how to live lives that glorify God in spite of the darkness we feel. I can honestly say I'm not sure I have ever felt spiritual battle as keenly as I did when I wrote these words. My prayer, and not just for myself, is that we will emerge as women who can say we trust our God fully and we are devoted to seeking Him in the midst of the fear.

As we work our way through different types of fears, I'll introduce you to some familiar and some not-so-familiar faces in the hopes that you might see a glimpse of yourself.

In the past few years I have had to come face to face with my greatest fears, and while I can't say it hasn't been incredibly hard, I can say this:

I believe Him, and I'm still standing.

Coming through some of my worst nightmares has given me an opportunity to trust Him in a way I have never needed to, and that solace walks me through the shadows day after day. My prayer is that you will reach the end of this book and you will be reminded that you have a God who is not unaware of anything you fear. He doesn't mock you for it, and you don't get a failing grade because you have moments of doubt.

I hope you won't lie in bed wondering if you've been "good enough" anymore. You won't think your name is going to show up on the naughty list and you are going to be ridiculed for the gaps in your character.

All that to say, my deepest longing is for you to run after tomorrow like there is something waiting there for you, possible through the kind of love that sees past our fear.

And who knows?

You might just get pom-poms and a new hairstyle if you brave the hallway.

God, be with us as we journey together through our fears. Bless us with understanding, with peace, and with the wisdom to seek Your face when we start to lose our footing. Bless those who are reading with exactly what they need to take from these chapters, and inspire them to start moving toward a life that is filled with the mercy that satisfies our souls.

CHAPTER 1

SITTING BY THE WELL

FEAR OF THE "WHAT IF . . ."

By all accounts, she had done what she was supposed to do.

Hagar had conceived a son with Abraham at his wife Sarah's urging. Sarah believed that the only way to keep her husband's legacy alive was to have a maidservant become impregnated, and she told Abraham her plan. He went along with it, despite the fact that God had given him a promise that didn't include another woman.

Apparently God's plan wasn't materializing the way Sarah had expected it would, so she took matters into her own hands.

It's what we do when we fear, isn't it?

We grab a hold of it and shake our will into the corners that don't make sense.

Here's a conversation I have had with the Lord in about a million different ways over the years: "I heard You say that, God, but it seems like maybe You have forgotten that You did. It seems like maybe I need to do this in order for it to all fall into place, so I'm going to move on ahead of You and You can catch up to me at the next stop. Sound good?"

Many times I have done this in such subtle ways that it wasn't until much later that I was convicted of my own prodding and intervening. Underneath it all is the voice of Satan, wishing I would keep worrying, keep striving, keep manipulating everything I can get my hands on.

Sarah's plan didn't go exactly the way she hoped it would, and years later she found herself pregnant with a son and very jealous of the woman she had arranged to bear her husband's first son. So even after both Sarah and Abraham had acted out of fear and disbelief, God fulfilled his promise and gave them a son, Isaac. During a feast in celebration of Isaac, she sees Hagar's son Ishmael laughing, and that's it. She tells Abraham it's time for Hagar to hit the road with her son.

I am reminded often of the pains I have taken in my life to "help" God, and I imagine you can think of those times as well. We want to trust Him and we do to a certain extent. But then come those times when the world isn't making sense and we lean on our own strength as our minds wrestle with the question that drives the fear.

Where are You in this, God?

I believe that was Sarah's heart-question when she urged her husband to proceed with Hagar, and the great agony that followed must have left her broken.

I should have listened, God. I should have trusted You even when I couldn't see Your hand in my life . . . now look at this mess I've made . . .

All the times I have read this story in Genesis, I have seen myself in Sarah; I get tangled up in my own plans and then I hit a breaking point. The one I never paid as much attention to was Hagar. As I reread the passage recently I was mesmerized by this woman and her story. I spent quite a bit of time walking with her in her trials and I came away with a gift from the Lord which I pray will bless you as well if you have ever walked in the fear of the *"what if . . ."*

━━━━━━━━━

I have very detailed memories of being hospitalized for anxiety as a child. As early as two or three years old, I began to worry about things that children need not worry about. I would insist that my father walk me around the house when it was time for bed so that I could check to make sure the front door was locked, the stove was turned off, that my baby sister was breathing, etc. I was tormented, even then, by thoughts of what could happen to them if I wasn't vigilant. It grew worse as the months passed and my parents decided it would be a good idea for me to see a psychologist. Every week I had an appointment with a very nice lady and she asked me to draw certain pictures and then she would ask me to describe them.

I was a pretty smart kid, so I realized by the second week that she was way more interested in the ones where I looked sad and everyone else looked happy. I was already a people-pleaser so I knocked myself out.

She thought it was a window into my soul but the truth was if I made myself out to be an unhappy kid, my parents took me out to Mexican instead of Burger King.

We would sit in the big booth, them across from me, and discuss what had happened in the session that day. I would dip chips into salsa and tell them that she gave me crayons and I drew a picture of myself on the outside of the house instead of the inside with them. We placed our order and I went into detail about how "stick figure" Angela was running away and I had a sad face but everyone else in my family had a happy face.

"Why do you feel that way, hon?" My mother sipped her Coke, trying to figure out what she had done wrong.

Meanwhile I was convinced that if I could keep the conversation going through chimichangas, I was pretty much guaranteeing a shot at Mexican ice cream.

As much as I loved the attention, I'm not sure those early therapy sessions really did much other than give me a love for tacos and one-on-one time with my mom and dad. I specifically remember thinking it was silly to go in and draw pictures, because that was all make-believe. What I feared was *real*. And there wasn't anything that lady could do about those fears. The drawings were just drawings. In real life, lots of things could go wrong.

I would quiz my dad on what he would do if someone broke into our house in the middle of the night. We would go through all of these different scenarios to make me feel safe and then eventually I would fall asleep from the exhaustion of worry. I remember asking him to pick up some things around the house so I could judge how strong he was. He must have passed the test because eventually I asked him if he would be able to rip the toilet out of the bathroom floor if he needed to and he told me he didn't think it would get to that. I remember not being satisfied with that response, but I'm still not sure how the toilet came into the picture in the first place.

The fear didn't resolve itself with time, and when I was five or six, my parents decided I needed to be hospitalized. The room was small, with a little TV hanging from the corner and a dresser by the bed. The bed went up and down, which was my only entertainment when my mother stepped out to make phone calls. I pretended I was in the chair that they pumped up to cut my mom's hair at the beauty parlor, and then I acted like it was a roller coaster. It kept my thoughts busy for a little while but they always circled back around to the fact that I was still in a hospital bed. They did a lot of tests and fed me a lot of Popsicles while I was there, and although I don't know if I received an actual diagnosis, the consensus was that I started to develop an ulcer and my worrying was very severe and abnormal.

I hated being there. The worst part was being in the room alone. I would climb down off the big bed and tiptoe to the door, cracking it wide enough to look down the hallways and make sure nobody was looking. Then I would slide along the wall as quietly as I could until I was right up against the yellow line. The yellow line was a piece of tape that stretched across the hallway and was the boundary line for kids. We couldn't go past it in any circumstance, and being the rule-keeper I was, it never crossed my mind to step across it. I would get as close as I could, my toes pressed up against it, and listen for my mother's voice. I would hear her making phone calls from the pay phone, talking and crying as she shared what was going on with me. I fell asleep there on more than one occasion, and was carried back to my starched white bed sheets by one of the nurses.

They tried to comfort me but nothing was going to calm me down until my mother got back, so I made up counting games and stared at the flickering lights that danced around the room from the static on the TV.

I can see that little girl in my mind, too small to even tuck herself into bed, and I weep for the parts of childhood she missed. It's not that I didn't have a happy childhood, because by all accounts it was ideal. It's just that I couldn't let myself do anything fully, without abandon, the way a child should. There was too much at stake, even then. I had to be in charge or everything would fall apart.

One of the things that was the most difficult for me during that time was being away from my parents. I feared that something would happen and that I wouldn't be there to prevent it. Right before I began my second grade year, my father got a new job and we were relocated to Kobe, Japan. We lived in a hotel for several months as we house-hunted, and I have such fond memories of my mother humming and putting on her Oil of Olay cream. I would lay on my stomach, legs bent, feet dancing in the air while I asked her to describe each of the steps in her beauty ritual.

She was beautiful to me, but more urgently, she was fragile.

After a few weeks, it was time for me to start school. I threw up for several days in a row as the big red X's counted down the squares on the calendar. When the day finally came for me to start, I got into a taxicab with my mother and my sister and we started the half-hour drive to my new school. I sobbed the whole way, clutching her soft hands and begging her to let me go back to the hotel with her. I will never forget pulling up to the huge school, kids and chaos everywhere.

My sister kissed my mom and jumped out of the car to meet some new friends and her kindergarten teacher. I, on the other hand, wouldn't let go of the car handle, and I shook with fear.

She started to cry.

"Please, Mommy. Don't leave me. Don't leave me here. If something happens . . ." I buried my head in her lap and clutched the hem of her skirt.

"Sweetie, everyone goes to school. Look at your sister. She just ran over there and she's already laughing and playing with some new friends. There is nothing to be afraid of." Her fingers smelled like cigarettes and face powder.

I remember thinking that she was out of her mind for saying something like that. Nothing to be afraid of? Of course there were things to be afraid of. She could get hit by a car on the way home. She could get robbed in the hotel room. A plane could crash into her while she was crossing the street to fill her grocery cart.

Nothing to be afraid of? Ridiculous.

There's *everything* to be afraid of.

My fingers tightened as the possibilities grew larger than life in my head, and the panic took over as my legs started to kick. I told her I wasn't going to let go. The saddest part was that I wasn't necessarily afraid of what would happen to me while I played on the playground at school, but rather what would happen to mother in a taxicab without me. The responsibility I put on myself to keep those around me safe was already at a fevered pitch before I could read, and it wasn't going to change anytime soon.

After a few minutes, my mother motioned to the cab driver to go on back to the hotel. She told me that we were coming back the next day and that I would have to get out. She would keep me with her for one more day and that was it. I shook with relief, thanking her over and over again. I couldn't help but wonder if it was actually supposed to be the other way around; after all, I was protecting her.

As with all of the other fears I have dealt with in my life (and likely you in yours), the central issue is the feeling that you aren't in control. I guess that isn't really accurate—I should say it's the realization that you *aren't* in control.

For me, this has been especially hard in the area of protecting people I love from harm. I was certain as a seven-year-old that if I wasn't there, something bad could happen. And if it did, the responsibility would rest squarely on my shoulders for the rest of my life. That wasn't something I could live with.

Whenever I was invited to a sleepover, I would cry. I wanted to be friends with everyone and I knew they were going to have a ball, but it meant being away from my house for the night, which was unbearable. My parents always encouraged me to go, and assured me that they would come get me if I needed them to, even if it was the middle of the night. On a handful of occasions I gathered my pajamas, toothpaste, and a *Little House on the Prairie* book and allowed my mother to drop me off. This was kind of a flop for a few reasons. Namely that I always ended up going home before midnight and also because I was a sixth grader with a penchant for Laura Ingalls when I should have been focused on playing "Light as a feather, stiff as a board." Eventually word got around that I wasn't worth inviting unless you needed a good laugh.

I was the ultimate party pooper, and although I developed mechanisms that helped me over the years, the fear didn't go away. For the record, neither did my love of prairie life, which proved to be even more awkward as the years passed.

My father will tell you that even when I left for college I was haunted by what might happen in my absence. Over and over they would tell me they were fine, that everything was great, and that I didn't need to miss out on college life because I was worried about them. A few months after I left home, my cousin was killed in a car accident. I hadn't been close to him, but nonetheless I was rattled by his death, and all of the feelings I had tried to stuff down became overwhelming. See? It happened. It happened all around, and not just to other people. Now it was possible in my own family.

I went home for Christmas vacation and my parents knew I wasn't doing well. At that point I saw a psychiatrist who thought medication was the best option. Unfortunately, this particular doctor wasn't super concerned with dosage, and after several incidences of passing out and having seizures, I was checked into a hospital. They gradually weaned me off the medication, explaining that I was on about ten times the amount that I should be on for my height and weight. I was hospitalized for a week or so while they made sure I was stable, and then released me back into the environment that brought out my greatest fears.

This idea of "what if" looms larger than life for many of the women I know, and there are two sides to the "what if" coin that must be addressed to really recognize it as a stronghold.

The first is the idea that something might happen in the future, and the second is the fear that we made a poor decision in the past and life could have resulted differently.

Let's spend a little time talking about the latter as I'm sure some of these examples will resonate with you.

"What if I had listened to my instinct that the baby's movement had slowed down? Would she be here now?"

"What if I had stayed with my husband? Would my life be better?"

"What if I hadn't said those words? Would they have accepted me?"

"What if I had seen the signs that he wasn't doing well? Could I have prevented it?"

"What if I had stuck with graduate school? Would I have a better job?"

"What if I had been stronger in my convictions? Would I be stuck here now?"

I would hasten to say that very few days go by without each of us having a conversation with ourselves about "what might have been." It could be something as insignificant as wishing we had chosen a healthier breakfast, but the fact of the matter is we spend a huge portion of our lives looking back. This thinking can weigh us down with guilt, shame, regret, and fear.

I went to church with a dear woman who had lost a baby at 39 weeks gestation. She found me in the foyer after our church service, and through teary eyes, she told me that her son had died of a cord accident. It had been three years since the incident, but as she shared with me, she recalled the day before his death when she felt like his movement was different. Having already had two other children, she wasn't overly concerned about it and convinced herself he was just calm. By the next morning she was panicked. She went into the hospital, where she was told that her son was gone. She suffered through a full labor and delivery, only to hold her beautiful stillborn son a few hours later. When she returned home, she sat in his nursery and wept while she wondered "what if?"

Even as she shared this with me, she asked the question again. It had haunted her for all these years, and had shaken her faith to the core. She was desperate to go back to the moment she first felt the concern and do it all differently. I'm sure her mind played every potential scenario in the coming months as she dealt with the loss. Her marriage and her parenting had fallen by the wayside as she had spiraled into the abyss of possibilities. With each passing Christmas and anniversary came the nagging voice, taunting her to imagine how it all would have been different if she had gone in one day sooner.

It is so easy to fear we have ruined something beautiful.

So easy for us to believe that we held the keys to what was supposed to be and now we are destined to live among the ashes that remain. And more often than we care to admit, we step back into a situation where we think we can redeem the past, only to find that we have no more peace than we did before. We are powerless in changing it, but paralyzed by the sense that we have tainted the great canvas of our lives.

Years ago I knew a girl who was married with three children. From the outside you would have thought she had it made, but underneath it all she wondered if she had chosen the right man. Before she had met her husband, someone else had broken her heart and she hadn't ever really gotten over it. She ended up having an affair and leaving her husband because she longed to know what she might have missed.

She was so busy looking backwards that she bumped full-force into a future that was anything but what she wanted.

There is a difference in learning from past mistakes and ruminating over the million-and-one ways we might have done it better. I speak from experience when I tell you that nothing good can be gained from such thinking.

Will you sit with me for just a moment and think about a situation in your life you wish you had handled differently? Several come to mind for me even as I am writing, and I am tempted to fret over my decisions. I can feel a sense of fear rising up in me, a sense of panic that I have done more damage than can be repaired.

I feel it in my bones, this curiosity about what might have been. If I allow myself to drift back there, I can spend many sleepless nights caught in a web of doubt. I believe that Satan preys on these moments, taunting us with our own self-doubt, rejoicing as we replay things over and over, desperate for a different outcome. Scripture gives us powerful words about these thoughts, and I encourage you to find strength in them when you begin to wonder.

> "We demolish arguments and every pretension that sets itself up against the knowledge of God, and we take captive every thought to make it obedient to Christ." (2 Corinthians 10:5)

We can't go back to the waiting room, to the friend's house, to the moment where the door slammed behind us. What we can do is go to the throne of grace with our regret and let Jesus redeem it as only He can. Take it captive before it takes you. As soon as the thought comes, make a conscious decision to set it at the foot of the cross, and make a commitment that you will leave it there. Will you always do it perfectly? Probably not. But you will develop the strength that comes from leaving the weight with Someone who is equipped to carry it. You weren't made to walk through life with the stack of missed opportunities pressing you into the ground. Unless it is a thought that will spur you on to good action in the future, it isn't worth allowing back in. Pray as you release this to God, asking to help you submit to His authority and leadership as you move away from a life consumed with regret. In order to be released from the burden of sin in your past, make a point of repenting of it to the Lord as specifically as you are able.

I am someone who lives in a constant state of worry about the future, and it's something I have to commit to the Lord many times a day. I fear that He has somehow forgotten me and that I'm on my own. I take matters into my own hands but He reminds me that He hasn't gone anywhere. There is always a moment in time when I can feel His gentle voice reassuring me, but it's usually hindsight that brings relief instead of trust in the moment. I long to be a woman who walks in the moment God has given me, with full confidence in what's to come. I know it isn't always going to look the way I want it to, but I long to internalize the fact that He is never going to forsake me or take His hands off me.

Where are You, God?

Let's return to Hagar for a moment as we consider the ways we struggle through this fear.

She ran until she couldn't run anymore and then she fell to the ground in defeat.

She had been given a few things from Abraham as he sent her on her way but now she was face-to-face with the reality that she couldn't feed her son. She was desperate and alone, and I imagine she wondered why God would put her through all of this just to end up alone in the desert, watching her boy suffer. Knowing that he was going to die, she placed him in a bush and walked a few steps away. She closed her eyes, unable to witness the death of her only son as he starved.

God hears the boy crying out and an angel of the Lord spoke to her, saying, "What is the matter, Hagar?" (Genesis 21:17).

I'm going to go out on a limb and say He knew what was the matter.

The angel proceeds to tell her not to be afraid and that the Lord had heard her son crying.

Where are You, God?

His answer, gentle as rain, falls upon her.

I have heard him. I am here.

He allowed Hagar a glimpse of her son's future in that moment, and while we don't always have that benefit, we do have the voice that says "I have heard you." Sometimes we hear it more clearly than others, but it is there always.

I must have read this story dozens of times without recognizing the power of what happens next. Scripture tells us that God opens Hagar's eyes and she sees a well of water. Well that's handy. Wonder how in the world she missed that?

Take note of the fact that it *doesn't* say He dropped a well of water right next to her, but rather that He opened her eyes to see it.

Her circumstances didn't change.

Her awareness did.

I have read before that the Hebrew word for "sight" is very similar to the word for "fear," and it finally dawned on me.[1]

In her state of panic, I can imagine that she closed her eyes and made herself blind to whatever the Lord had in store for her. I recognize this same behavior in myself; I become convinced that the worst-case scenario is upon me and I better just give up. Not only do I surrender to it, I become an active participant in my own "worst-case scenario" as I cower behind a rock and anticipate the end.

This hit me like a ton of bricks. Such a simple sentence and yet it breathes life into me as I consider it. I hope it will do the same for you.

Hagar sat in full anticipation of her son's death, and instead of looking to what God had given her, she surrendered to the fear.

Is it possible that the well is right beside you but you haven't seen it because your head is hung in grief? Are you so focused on what you think is missing that you don't see what is present? Maybe you need to ask the Lord to illuminate what it is He wants you to see. It's possible that what you have seen as the end of the road is actually an opportunity to open your eyes and see something you haven't.

I don't want to walk through this life with my eyes closed, convinced that God has forgotten me. I have begun to pray against this, asking the Lord to open my eyes as I cower from a fate I have imposed on myself. I have so many friends who say the same, and I don't disagree that their circumstances feel grim. With many of their husbands out of work and so many unknowns, I understand the fear of not being able to see where God is working. It sounds glib of me to say that, unless you know that I have been in situations where I was sure I wouldn't be rescued and the helplessness nearly did me in. I speak not as one who has merely believed in the unlikely miracle for others, but rather as one who has drunk deep of the well herself. Things I never thought would bloom in that desert soil have been the most spectacular, life-changing moments of my life. I think it's also worth noting that I wasn't always nourished in the way I was expecting or wanting. Sometimes it comes in a form we don't recognize at the time. It's only in the looking back that we realize God's hand was in it. He provided for us when we thought we wouldn't see the light of day again.

It's hard to say I will never worry again, and you may feel the same way. Remember that the God of Hagar is still listening to our cries, despite evidence you may feel is to the contrary. When you find yourself in a situation that seems hopeless, remember the woman who mourned a son she wasn't going to lose. Remember the moment the Lord opened her eyes to see His provision, waiting there for her all the while.

Take heart, friend.

Drink deep of the faithfulness of God in the hopes that the next time you face insurmountable odds you won't cower in fear. You will learn to keep your eyes open to what God is doing, always confident that the Lord of Hagar loves you just as He loved her.

———

Lord, I believe You are the well-maker, but I also believe You are the eye-opener. I pray that each person reading these words will ask You to reveal Yourself in a personal and profound way, and that they will see hope in a place that was barren with fear. I pray that in every circumstance we will choose You over hopelessness, and that we will know even to the core of our being that You are working on our behalf. Let us remember to keep our eyes, our hearts, and our desires open to what You have in store for our lives. I pray our days will be filled with gratitude as You turn the unlikely into the obvious. Lord, we love You . . . unspeakably so. Thank You . . .

CHAPTER 2

FOUNDATIONS OF THE WORLD

FEAR OF REJECTION, ABANDONMENT, AND BETRAYAL

═══════════════════════

He had it all. He and his family were healthy, he was the wealthiest man around, and life looked the way it was supposed to. It's easy to trust God in the sunshine of life, isn't it?

In the span of a few moments, Job is told that he has lost valuable animals, workers, and his sons. Shortly after that he is stricken with disease, and his wife suggests that he just curse God and die. He rebukes her and declares His love for the Master, telling her that they should praise Him for the good days and the bad.

We don't hear much more about his wife, so I'm thinking he wasn't all that excited about her counsel.

Job also has several friends who are full of answers; unfortunately none of them are God's answers. In a sea of chaos and destruction, Job faces the fear that threatens to destroy him.

Has my God abandoned me?

It cuts us to the quick as we think of all the earthly examples we have of abandonment, betrayal, and rejection. It is a terrifying thing to put your full weight into someone, only to be exposed as the fool. It may have begun in childhood, when we felt like we weren't the "favorite." It may have been senior year in high school as the music blasted and all the kids around you danced and you stared at the floor wondering why you spent this much money on a dress that nobody would see. Maybe it was the night your husband told you he had met someone else. You might have watched one of your own children go down a destructive path, turning his back to you and the God you long for him to love.

And in each of these moments, whether you realize it or not, your image of God has been tested. You know He would never leave you, even if the rest of the world did.

At least, you don't *think* He would.

As we watch Job shout to the heavens we are reminded of our own circumstances, our own memories of being wronged. If you have blood pulsing through your veins I would hasten to say that you have had a conversation with God at some point in time that resembles the one we read about between the Lord and Job. Job is desperate with anger and he can't understand why the God he loves faithfully has allowed this to happen.

I can certainly say I have been there.

You may not only have the fear of social situations but, more than that, a true fear that someone could harm you physically, emotionally, or mentally. If you have a past filled with people who didn't treat you the way they should have, you have a unique hurdle as far as trusting those around you. The fear of other people (whether their words, their actions, their secrets about you, and so on) fits itself into several different categories depending on the nature of the situation. These are the fears that make us think we looked foolish, or we trusted too much, or maybe were naïve in thinking we had finally gotten it right, only to be told we were all wrong. These are the fears that say, "You can't trust me to be what you need me to be . . ." and "Don't rely on anyone but yourself . . ."

As I go through seasons of my life where others have hurt me and let me down, I can see the way my image of God was affected. It all lends to that overarching sense that you are your only ally, and anyone else (including Him) will fail you.

Let me go back a little ways, though. These patterns of fear didn't happen overnight, but rather, for me, through years of fighting the voice in the back of my head that said, *"You should never trust this way . . . it will only lead to hurt . . ."*

—————

It was Thanksgiving Day in 1988 and I was an awkward twelve-year-old. Junior high school is scary enough in its own right, but having it be my first year back in the States after several years in Japan made it even worse. I didn't understand fashion at all, which is evidenced by my school photo that year, complete with a Victorian style dress and crimped hair. In case you're wondering, that's the surefire way to have pencils thrown at the back of your head while you ride home on the bus.

I was paralyzed by the culture shock, and as hard as I tried, I was simply an outcast. I was the girl who wore six ponytails simultaneously (Yes, that was a trend in Japan. Here? Not so much) and denim sailor dresses (stop laughing). The sad part was that I had spent so many hours overseas watching *Anne of Green Gables* that I had become convinced that I was one French braid away from finding a bosom buddy. I tried to talk to the girls in my class and really felt like I was making progress when one of the popular girls complimented my outfit. I found out later that the word "clash" didn't actually mean she was impressed.

After school, I would run in the door, throw my backpack on the floor, and race up the stairs before my mother could ask how my day was. What kid wants to tell her family that she's the laughingstock of sixth grade? Not me.

But this Thanksgiving was different. I had received a call from two girls in my class. They both lived in my neighborhood and wanted to let me know that they were going to be starting a ballet school soon and they were looking for teachers. They were hoping to get a few girls our age to teach younger kids, and the fact that I had a few dance lessons under my belt (read: clogging. Seriously, stop laughing), they wanted me to come in for an audition. I got the specifics and ran to find my parents and informed them that I was going to need a quick ride to a place where I could get some ballet shoes and a leotard. I believe I also bought tap shoes and legwarmers, just in case.

I was an overachiever, what can I say?

Despite my gangly legs and odd proportions, I was actually a fairly good dancer. I really felt like this might be my chance to break into the inner circle. I was petrified I was going to mess up so I stayed up late and practiced all of the basic moves they told me to know. When they called the next day and asked me to head over I felt ready. I put on my new dance outfit, legwarmers and all.

"Do you want me do drive you down there, hon?" my mom asked.

"No. I think I'll just walk. It's not that far, you know?"
She nodded.

"Are you nervous?" Her eyes looked like she knew the answer.

"Well, I just don't want to make a mistake and look like I don't know what I'm doing. I just want it to go perfect."

"I'm sure it will, sweetie." She smiled and I wanted to believe her.

I slipped my dance bag over my shoulder and walked into the coldness of November.

It took me a good fifteen minutes to get there and when I did they were already working on a bar routine, so I just sat and watched. I had decided the night before that blurriness would be a worthy consequence of looking cooler, so I slipped my pink plastic glasses into their case in my bag. I smiled really big and tried to show them I was interested. I knew that was what I was supposed to do to make friends.

At least that's what it said in the book my mom bought me.

Finally they asked me to stand up and I made my way over to where they were.

"Hi guys. I just wanted to um, you know, um." My hands were clammy and I couldn't think of what I wanted to say next.

They were looking at me like my head was on fire.

"I just wanted you to know I'm really glad you asked me to come. I appreciate the chance to be a dance teacher."

They smiled at each other and then at me.

"Well then, let's get started." Margaret motioned for Carrie to start the music.

"Okay, just do like this." Margaret went through the basic ballet positions, which I had practiced and got through with no problem. Then she started doing some toe pointing and bar work and I just did my best to keep up.

This went on for about a half hour. No feedback, no talking. Just them watching and evaluating me. At the end of it they just said they were done and I didn't want to leave without feeling like I had given it my best shot.

I'm pretty sure I learned *that* from the book my dad had bought me.

"Um, do you guys want to see me do the splits? I can do them right side and left side but I can't do middle ones." I bit my lip and waited for the verdict, squinting in case there was a subtle response I should pick up on.

"No, Angela. I think we got exactly what we needed. Thanks so much for coming over." They smiled at me. In fact, it was more than a smile. They were so happy I thought for sure they were going to choose me. I thanked them again and then started up the stairs that led to the front door. Full of confidence and grateful for my first real opportunity to be included, I headed up the stairs and out of the house. They turned on the radio and did the choreography to "Walk Like an Egyptian" as I waved good-bye again from the top of the stairs. Those arm moves were cool. Just like Egyptians. I would have to ask about those before the next dance class. This was going to be awesome. I breathed a sigh of relief and headed out, my hands digging in my bag for my glasses so I could see where I was going.

Just before the door closed completely behind me I heard the girls burst into laughter. It was hard to make out all the words, but in bits and pieces I heard, "She actually believed it!!! What an idiot. Like we would ever call her even if we did have a ballet school. LOSER!" followed by raucous laughter and hand-slapping.

The cold wind hit me in the face as I realized what was happening. I stared at the ground and my glasses slid down my sweaty nose.

There was no ballet school.

No need for leotards, legwarmers, or hope. Just a cruel chance to make the weird girl walk in the freezing cold to her shame. As I walked away from the house I was crying and Margaret's mom was pulling in the driveway. She rolled down her window and asked if I was okay and if she could take me home.

I nodded no. No to both.

I picked up my bag and my embarrassment and I ran all the

way home, tears stinging and legs exhausted. I ran back to the warm house with the fireplace and the Macy's Day Parade. Back to where I fit in no matter what color my socks were or what books I loved to read. Back to where I could be me. And in another few days I would have to return to the place that reminded me I was different. This pattern continued for most of my junior high and high school years, complete with a cheerleading try-out that ended with a cartwheel where my shirt came over my head and I flashed all the judges. (I didn't make it that year.)

We've all been there, haven't we? Well, if you haven't, just pretend along with the rest of us for a bit. Maybe it wasn't in school or even in such a public way, but that subtle conversation that is happening around you but not including you. You're on the periphery and you know it. The sting of rejection is brutal, and for many of us it leads to avoiding any situation where it could happen again.

I know many people who have walked away from the pos-sibility of love or even friendship because the price would be too high to pay if it didn't work out. I can't say I haven't struggled with that myself. People who meet me will tell you that I'm social and outgoing, but it isn't really true. I'm just trying to make sure I don't stick out enough to be made fun of. There's a good chance I will be humming "Walk Like an Egyptian" as you walk away, wondering if I have made a fool of myself.

It is so hard to love people in full expectation of them loving you back. You put it all out there, knowing that the other person always has the decision of what to do with your affection.

Maybe you've been there? If so, there's a woman I want you to meet. Her name is Leah and she has been rejected plenty of times. She's also not unfamiliar with the pain that comes from being related to someone who *wasn't* rejected. I can imagine what her life might have looked like as she grew up with her beautiful sister Rachel. She was the elder of the two, and we are told that she wasn't particularly attractive. Scripture says she had "weak" eyes, possibly meaning she was cross-eyed or that her eyes weren't attractive in a physical sense.

The book of Genesis chronicles Jacob meeting Rachel and falling in love with her. He decided that she was to be his wife and he went to her father to ask permission to marry her. Laban agreed to the marriage but tells Jacob he must work for seven years in order to have her. Jacob gladly does the work in order to have his precious bride. In fact he is so in love that Scripture tells us the time seemed to fly by and the night of their wedding finally came.

The morning after Jacob married Rachel, he realized that he actually hadn't married Rachel, but rather her older sister Leah. Laban had plotted to marry off the older, not-so-adorable sister first and then make Jacob work another seven years to get Rachel.

I'm just going to go ahead and say that this had to be a less-than-ideal beginning to a marriage.

Can you imagine?

At some point Laban had to come to Leah and inform her that this was his plan. I wonder how he approached that?

"Leah, hey. Listen. You aren't beautiful like Rachel and the only way we are going to marry you off is to trick someone into being your husband. The good news is that the guy really loves your sister, so eventually you all will get to fight for his love as his wives."

Ballet school is suddenly looking up.

I've also wondered about the conversation he must have had with Rachel, telling her that she needed to find something else to do while he fooled the man she loved into marrying her desperate sister. Did she protest? Could she? Did she watch from afar, all the while stifling her cries as she watched it unfold?

When all was said and done, Jacob did marry Rachel, who was obviously his favorite. I bet you can relate to this next part, and I really hope we can flesh this out in our lives and allow the Lord to convict us where we need to be.

Leah can't win him over with looks, so she comes up with another plan to make him love her.

Reading what you have so far, you can probably guess that it didn't work. In fact, Scripture says that despite the fact that she bore Jacob six sons and a daughter, he hated her.

He *hated* her.

I haven't specifically done that, but I've done plenty in the way of trying to make someone love me for the wrong reasons. How about you? Have you ever feared rejection so badly that you used your money to win someone over? What about your body? Your talents? Your connections? Something else?

If you did, I can pretty much tell you what happened after that. You gave away a piece of yourself and in the end you never even got what you set out to get.

Neither did Leah.

Women who lived in this time period were lauded for the number of sons they could provide their husbands, and while Rachel was barren, the Lord blessed Leah's womb. I'm sure that every time she realized she was pregnant she thought things were going to change with Jacob. In fact, her son's names tell us volumes about her hopes. She named her first son Reuben (meaning, "see, a son") and explained, "It is because the LORD has seen my misery. Surely my husband will love me now." (Genesis 29:32). Shortly after, she had another son and named him Simeon (meaning "one who hears") to recognize that God had given her another baby because her husband didn't love her. A third boy was born to her, and she named him Levi (meaning "attached"), expressing the hope that her husband would finally feel attached to her now that she has provided him another son. He didn't.

Whenever I'm reading Scripture, I love to imagine I am there to retain the information and really experience it. In this story

I find my thoughts drifting to the birth of Leah's third son, as she cradles him for the first time and his tiny, waxy little body holds the promise of winning over her husband. I wonder if Jacob ever looked upon her with any sense of pride or gratitude as she showed him another son. If he did, we aren't told. Just a woman, sweating through the agony of childbirth with the solitary thought "This will be the one . . ." only to be discouraged again and reminded that she has been rejected.

At some point after the birth of Levi, Leah must have realized that she wasn't going to get the love she longed for so desperately. The next time she gave birth she was focused on the Lord instead of her husband's favor, and she named her fourth son Judah (meaning "praise") and said, "This time I will praise the LORD" (Genesis 29:35).

So not only was she no longer trying to win over Jacob, but she was expressing gratitude to the Lord for her newest child. Quite a shift in perspective, isn't it? She made the conscious decision to stop trying to please man and pursue what she desired in favor of praising God for blessing her with children. In a sense, she surrendered her will for her life, accepting her husband's rejection. There is power in relying on the Lord's view of us over the opinions of everyone else. I know from experience that there is a lot of agony, too. I don't dismiss it, and I'm not proposing you should either. It would be wonderful to think we aren't ever going to be abandoned, rejected, scorned, or ridiculed again but it isn't likely. On the other hand, we know that the Lord will do none of these things, and even when we feel unloved by our neighbors, we must seek the arms of God. There is rest there as we focus on the fact that it is His nature to love us well, and we need not fear that He will leave us stranded. There is a glorious feeling in being able to believe He truly is enough, but most often we don't turn to Him in that way when the world is being good to us.

I don't know that I do a great job of resting and depending

on Him fully unless I am pressed against a wall, out of options, begging for relief. I can sometimes grow distant from God when I get so close to someone else that I feel like maybe that person can take a little of His responsibility or accomplish some of the things in my life that I should truly get solely from Him.

I remember walking through a season where this was particularly evident to me. I was a newlywed and I believed that my new husband Todd had hung the moon, relying on him to help me process every emotion, being every person I needed, and depending on him in a way that I allowed to hinder my relationship with the Lord. I simply decided that I would take my focus off of God being my Provider because I had this adorable, capable, dependable man who was taking good care of me. I didn't feel the need for God the way I should have.

Well, the Lord loves an opportunity to draw us close to Him, doesn't He? Several months into our marriage we found out I was pregnant with twins and Todd was on the road quite a bit at that time. I threw up all day (and night) long, crying myself to sleep because I felt so alone. I would wait for Todd to call me after his concerts and when he did I would unload my mental artillery and wait for him to come up with a solution. My mental health pretty much depended on him picking the right thing to say. I was a wreck. No matter how hard he tried, or how much he wanted to be enough, he couldn't be.

He wasn't meant to be.

When we depend on others to be our God, we strike out on a couple different levels. We burden them with blame for their lack of ability and we forfeit what God could have done if we would have honored Him the way we should have.

I imagine Leah weeping night after night as she wrestled with the fact that her love was sharing a bed with her sister while she cared for his children. As much as I sympathize with Leah, I admire her resolve as she committed her life to praise in the valley. The way she chose her God over her husband and set out on a new path to bring Him glory.

Those of you who are familiar with this particular story probably know that from the line of Judah comes our Christ. The Lord chose the woman who had been rejected to be part of the lineage that brought the Redeemer Himself. What a beautiful, profound image for all of us who are tempted to believe that our pain can't be transformed into glory.

What we see as someone failing us is the chance to see God refuse to do so. Sometimes I think He allows us to go down our little bunny-trails of expectation with others because we have to learn the hard way in order for it to be real to us. He is the only One Who can love us in a way that truly satisfies our souls.

This is the goal. That we should be striving every day to make Jesus the One we want to please and honor more than any other. And if it were that easy to change lifelong patterns with one sentence, I would be all for it. Realistically it isn't that simple. Some of us have walked through times of crippling rejection, and to say that we just need to snap our fingers and change sounds flippant. So how do we get there? How do we turn the corner from fear of rejection to peace and trust no matter the situation? Can we manage that in this lifetime? I think we can make great strides.

So often we base our self-worth on the chatter going on around us instead of the Lord Himself. That in itself can be crippling, but imagine what it would be like to put your full weight into Him and then feel like maybe you had really been duped. What if you walked with Him day in and day out, only to become fearful that you had been abandoned and deceived?

Those of us who have fears of rejection, abandonment, or betrayal with people around us will no doubt have those same concerns about God. The truth is, we have gotten used to being disappointed in ourselves for being so vulnerable. We assume, even if unconsciously, that God is another rung on the ladder of misplaced trust.

He is not.

Scripture is very clear in saying that He will not abandon us, and we must know Him well enough to believe Him. The world is not going to teach us how to love God; only God can do that. Don't believe the lie that Satan longs to use against you; God has not, and will not, forsake you.

Ever.

Period.

You'll recall the discussion about Job from earlier. Interestingly, when Job goes to the Lord with his anger and confusion, God asks him a simple question that will rock our world to the core even to this day. At first glance it may seem callous that in the midst of Job's suffering, the best God can do to comfort him is to ask, "Where were you when I laid the earth's foundation?" (Job 38:4).

Well that's one way to end a conversation.

And He doesn't stop there. In fact, He goes on to ask Job over thirty more questions in this chapter alone.

I'm thinking Job didn't feel real solid about his case when God finished His little pep talk.

I love the Message version of Job's response; it says, "I'm speechless, in awe—words fail me. I should never have opened my mouth! I've talked too much, way too much. I'm ready to shut up and listen" (Job 40:3–5).

It seems like a pretty decent response.

This conversation would be comical if it didn't hit such a nerve in me. I get hurt and I immediately hurl my side of things to the Lord, ignoring any response He might be trying to fit in as I rage on about the unfairness of it all. In my haste I can forget a very simple truth that would serve me well when I'm convinced the world needs to revolve around my disappointment.

"Where were you when I laid the foundation, Angie?"

I imagine Job felt a bit sheepish, and maybe even hurt by the chastening, but the truth is that it was a speech made in love. God wasn't trying to defeat Job, but rather to remind him that He had done a pretty good job of setting up shop Himself.

Why does that always amaze me? I have no issues believing He set the waves of the ocean into their course, or that He breathed life into being, but as far as this situation with someone who broke me? I can't imagine why He would make Himself small enough to care. My mind says, "They have rejected me, so I guess *You* have as well."

But that is *my* error in thinking, not based in any reality from the Lord.

And in the event that I don't remember that, I have a question to answer, and maybe you do too. Before I speak, I pray I will remember that He is the Beginning and the End, and He doesn't take it lightly when I blame Him for my misconceptions. He longs for us to love Him, and the more I rely on Him, the stronger I find Him. In times where I have faced the sting of rejection and the agony of feeling forgotten, I have found the Love of my life faithful. That is the steady foundation for all other relationships, and the more I find my balance in Him, the less I will fret about what the world says.

It is a precious place to be, and I pray you will trust Him and depend on Him when you are tempted to believe you aren't worth it. Remember a man named Job and a simple question that puts it all in perspective. Just as the Lord placed the stars in the heavens, He knows every second of your life from the moment of conception to the day you will see Him face to face. Every second.

Once there was a little girl who wanted to be a ballerina.

But even more than that, she wanted to be liked.

When the world told her she could do neither, He walked her home and asked her to dance one cold November day. There have been many pauses in the music, and many missteps on my part, but I am convinced that He loves me in spite of them.

He saw what they never could, and I'm still dancing because of it.

―――――――

Thank You, Lord. You are not unaware of what it feels like to be persecuted, rejected, and betrayed. I am so grateful for a God who stooped low enough to feel the way humanity aches. You remind me constantly that despite what my mirror, my friends, or my neighbors choose to think about me, I was worth You dreaming me up. May I live a life worthy of the King who spoke me into being, eyes fixed on Him, heart steadfast in love, and always aware of His presence in the times I feel forgotten and discarded. You are the Joy of my life, Jesus. May it always be so . . .

CHAPTER 3

CHASING HIS HEM

FEAR OF BEING FOUND OUT

═══════════════════════════

She walks through a crowd of people, eyes down and heart pounding.

She doesn't want them to know.

She is hiding something that could ruin her, and if she can figure out a way to just slip through the people and get to Him, she may be healed. That's what she's after, anyway.

Healing.

She doesn't want to be noticed, to be called out, to be identified. She just wants to touch Him from the shadows, all the while keeping her secret to herself. It was shameful, and she couldn't bear the thought of everyone knowing she wasn't what she seemed.

She sees her chance, and immediately she moves toward Him. Just a touch of His cloak and it will all be over.

No more shame, no more hiding, no more secrecy. The crowd was all around her and she blended in with the throngs of people as they clamored to be near Him.

His hem, my freedom. I believe He can save me from this . . .

In an instant she reached out, felt the cloth in her hands, and was miraculously healed. She must have known it.

But it wasn't exactly as she had planned.

There, in the chaos of people, He stopped.

I suspect she panicked as she considered what might happen next.

"Who touched me?" He asked.

I can imagine the way her blood must have run cold.

She had been discovered.

It hadn't happened the way she had pictured it . . . a stranger just reaching out anonymously and sneaking a blessing.

He knew who had touched Him.

And He knew why.

He asked because He wanted her to speak up and to identify herself in spite of her fear. He clearly wasn't trying to humiliate her, but I wonder if she felt like He was going to. As He waited for her response, the people began to murmur innocence. *Not me, not me, not me . . .*

I wonder if she panicked. I wonder if she was too desperate to even care at that point. All eyes were on her, and she realized she was not longer hidden. She fell at His feet, shaking with fear as she identified herself. There was no point in keeping up the charade.

She realized she was caught.

Do you?

━━━━━━━

Jenny was always the center of attention. She walked into a room and lit the place up with her infectious smile and calm, cool demeanor. I always envied her because she had this ability to be completely comfortable in her own skin no matter what situation she was in. She was one of the most gifted women I have ever known, not just in her career but also as a mother and wife. Her home was filled with antiques she had collected over the years and it was always clean and inviting. I used to walk through her doorway and fight feelings of inadequacy. I would beat myself up about what I was going to go home to, including a husband I was in a disagreement with, loads of laundry I had neglected to finish, and no plan for dinner.

As often as possible, I suggested eating out on our lunch dates. It kind of leveled the playing field a little.

I couldn't understand how she kept it all together and it honestly broke my heart. I would taunt myself with thoughts like, *Todd would have been so much better off with someone like that . . .* or *I will never be creative enough to inspire my children that way . . .*

And going to her house for her kids' birthdays was salt in the wound. The house was decorated to the hilt; everything fitting in with whatever the theme was that year. And the thing was, it wasn't pretentious at all. She was one of the most gracious, kind, warm hostesses you could ever imagine and she just made everyone feel right at home. I would have felt a little better about it if she had run around all frazzled and snapping her fingers, but she never did. She just had it so together and it seemed effortless.

Needless to say, the "Dora the Explorer" banner I got at the grocery store to celebrate Kate's birthday looked pathetic a few weeks later, so I went through a phase where I decided I was going to give my inner Suzy Homemaker a whirl. I baked from scratch. I wore lipstick every day, even if I was doing laundry (starched, ironed, and perfectly hung, naturally). I bought at least ten cookbooks to display in the kitchen and I prayed that God would help me become a woman just like Jenny.

I don't remember how long it lasted but I know it wasn't long. I also know I burned a lot of food.

We were set to have a play date and I convinced myself to broach the topic while I was there. Surely she had a book hidden away that would give me all of her secrets and teach me how to do it. Either that or we could start some weekly meetings where she would inspire me to be a better woman. Whatever the case, she had what I needed and I intended to get it.

The conversation that ensued will stay with me for the rest of my life.

We both sat cross-legged on the floor, toys scattered around us as the kids played. We caught up for a few minutes and as the kids wandered into the backyard I decided to initiate the conversation.

"Jen, can I ask you something?" She nodded and sipped her coffee while I struggled to find the right opening sentence.

"How do you do all of this? I mean, your house, your job, your kids—everything. I really look up to you and I want to work on this stuff in myself."

There wasn't really any response so I kept going. It was hard to gauge what she was thinking and I figured it was because she couldn't imagine anyone had never cooked their way through Betty Crocker's plaid marvel.

"Do you cook like this every night? Because that is incredible, Jen. I try so hard and it just doesn't work, you know?" I gestured into the kitchen and in the time it took for me to glance in there and finish my sentence, her eyes had filled with tears.

"I'm a sham, Angie."

I stared at her, not knowing what she meant or what I was supposed to say in return. She buried her head in her hands and I could see her shoulders shaking as she explained that she was a mess and that for years she had been doing everything she could to keep up the pretense.

We've all heard this story a million times, I know. It wasn't what we thought, she wasn't who we thought, and on and on. But this was different—this was shocking.

After several minutes of me listening (and not understanding much because she was just trying to breathe through her words) I finally said, "Jenny I want you to tell me what it is you feel like you need to hide. I'm not going to love you less and it sounds like there are some things you need to get off your chest."

She wiped her face with the back of her hand and asked if I wanted a cup of coffee. I did. In fact, we went through four cups each as we talked for the next several hours. At one point she told me she had really struggled with anger, and when I asked her to explain, she told me that her husband spent his weekends patching up drywall from where she had punched through the walls. She had thrown a heavy metal toy in the direction of her son, not intending to harm him but rather to scare him. She said that when it brushed his cheek she knew she needed to get help before she put anyone in danger.

We made a lot of progress over the next several months and I think she was really able to see that her life behind closed doors wasn't as alienating as she feared. She told me on many occasions that she felt like a weight had been lifted off her when she finally shared with me, and after that she was able to get the help she needed. She found a great Christian counselor and started to tackle her problem with anger.

I believe that Satan was disappointed that he lost some of his foothold on her one summer day in Nashville, when she let me into the world she had spent years hiding. I am amazed at the number of women who have felt safe in contacting me and sharing the fact that they fear being "found out."

One woman shared a devastating story about her feelings on motherhood, even going so far as to confess that she sometimes fantasized about leaving her house and never coming back. She was overwhelmed with parenting and believed she was a poor mother and that her children would be better off without her. The fact that she even had these thoughts was so alarming to her that she made herself into a monster in her mind. She was ashamed, never having told anyone, and she was certain I was going to chalk her up as a nutcase.

Here's what she didn't know.

I had dozens of e-mails from other women saying the *exact same thing.*

Bound by their fears of being exposed as imposters, these women have kept secrets that they believed would ruin them. And there were patterns I couldn't help but see as I read—faith, family, friends, careers, etc.—all areas in which women assumed they were alone in their struggles. From where I was sitting I could see all of their words along with everyone else's, but they didn't have the benefit of that viewpoint. Just their own keyboard and the hope that they wouldn't be judged by the contents of the message they wrote. It's a microcosm of what the Lord must see every day as He watches His daughters walk through life without seeing the hearts of the women around them.

One woman said that although she was a pillar in her church as a women's Bible study leader, she questioned her own salvation. There have been dozens of people who said that people saw them as much more spiritual than they felt they actually were.

Many have said that their marriages were a sham and that they were exhausted from trying to keep up the façade. Some were more severe than others, but they nearly all told the same story: "It isn't what it looks like, and if people only knew the real story . . ."

I think that one of the ways we combat this fear is by allowing ourselves to continue the thought to the end. If you knew this, then what? Well, maybe you would look at me differently. You might not respect me. You could decide not to let your kids come play anymore, or decide to want to drop out of a church group because you can't see past it. Okay, there's a step. Let's keep going.

What if you tell everyone and they see that I'm just a shadow of who they thought I was. I'll never be able to walk into church with them looking at me, knowing my secrets. I'll be humiliated beyond recovery, and my life will be ruined forever.

Okay, that's kind of dramatic, don't you think? More than likely, the places you go in your imaginary scenario are never going to happen. But what if they did? Well, I guess that would stink, but I still think life would go on. It isn't really the end of the world to feel like somebody thinks of you differently; in fact I think it's a pretty good barometer of how much they truly loved you in the first place.

It's so interesting to put ourselves on the other side of the equation, though, where we tend to be accepting and loving of another person's weaknesses. We don't expect them to respond that way toward us, but we know it to be true in ourselves. I have had dear friends tell me about the shame they bear and I know that when I see them, I don't even think about it. To me, who they are (really) is not based on a single uncharacteristic action, or a part of themselves covered in shame. I see the whole person, and I don't judge based on errors or weaknesses. I want to help them make better decisions, and try to give counsel that lends itself to strengthening character, but I don't hold it against them.

I became a believer as a twenty-four-year-old, so I had a wealth of life experience as a nonbeliever. I didn't grow up with the Bible-based lens of what was wrong and right, and I naturally had a personality that pretty much accepted everyone for who they were. While my perspective on right and wrong behavior has changed in light of to what I believe God calls us, I can honestly say that I can love a person well despite any behaviors I believe are wrong.

I think one of the reasons we, as Christians, fear baring our souls for each other is that we know the person may try to play God instead of trying to love us the way God commands. I have seen firsthand the way that people throw out sentences and rules from Scripture with the intention of criticizing and issuing judgment, all without the love that Christ urges us to bestow on one another. There is such a difference between genuine empathy and trying to help guide someone in their walk and simply making them feel like they are a moral failure. I can think of several times that I really opened up about something I was struggling with and it was met by a posture and spirit of judgment coupled with Bible verses. I want the Bible verses, but in a spirit of love and grace.

Another fear that many of us have is that we will let people down and not meet their expectations of us. I think so many of us feel like the real "us" will be exposed when we don't rise up to what someone else thinks we should be. So many of us feel burdened by our perceptions of the expectations of others. We often live our lives trying to avoid letting people down. I'll be transparent with an example on this one. After my blog started gaining momentum, every now and then someone would stop me when I was out because they recognized me. Immediately I would be totally paranoid about what my children were doing, how I was dressed, whether or not the person thought I was engaged in the conversation, and on and on and on. I made myself sick with worry because I felt like people had an image of me that I couldn't live up to. I would walk away from those conversations and say to myself, "Well, now they know. One more reader lost, I guess."

The sad thing is it had nothing to do with the other person; it was totally in my head. But that fear was so intimidating, and it has taken me a long time to get to a place where I don't feel like I have to live up to everything people want to believe about me. It looks different in each of our lives, but either consciously or unconsciously, we can become so caught up in what we think people are seeing in us that we lose sight of who we are. As a result, we may begin to shut down socially and decide that building walls makes more sense than a broken heart.

As a result, many of us talk about the weather at Bible study instead of the fight we had with our teenage daughter, knowing that we might be labeled the overprotective parent, or the one who can't control her own children. And long after the issue is resolved, we will still be seen as the one who messed up. The labels we create (and dwell on) for each other are killing our chance for genuine community, and we are missing the best part of each other.

How about you? What do you think people could find out about you that would destroy the image they have of you?

If you're anything like me, you can immediately think of several things you believe would ruin people's perceptions of you. You might even say you spend more time "presenting" yourself rather than being present. Anyone?

Recently I was being considered to speak at a women's event and I really wanted them to like me. I think I was actually more concerned with them liking me than them asking me to speak at the event. I went to the mall and spent a ridiculous amount of money on a new outfit, makeup, and perfume that I didn't need. I practiced my "look" when I got home, asking Todd to vote on the potential outfits. He nodded at all of them, complimenting me on my choices, but obviously unsure of what he was supposed to be doing to make me feel better. I had delivered a baby a few months before and still wasn't fitting into my pre-maternity clothes so my self-esteem was faltering. Between that and the hormones, it wasn't a whole lot of fun to try and look pretty.

I finally picked one I thought made me look much cooler than I actually am and I reached in the goody bag from the makeup store to see if I could re-create what they had done to my face.

I was giving Todd a running commentary as I unloaded the supplies and I realized when I got to the bottom of the bag that they had forgotten to put an item in there. I grabbed the receipt, panicked, thinking maybe I had dropped it in the car or on the way into the house, but it wasn't even listed. I can't fully explain why, but this was a breaking point for me. I literally sat down on the floor of the bathroom and started crying, sure that the whole weekend was ruined. And it wasn't just that I hadn't gotten my makeup. I had it in my head that all of these things would come together and magically trick them into thinking I was beautiful and well put together. I didn't feel beautiful, so I was just going to fake it.

I hung my hopes of acceptance on a tube of concealer. (Hello, irony. Thanks for showing up. *Again*.)

And admit it, so have you.

It might not have been in the form of makeup, but you were convinced that whatever it was would be your saving grace.

I know a woman who flashes her 4-carat diamond ring everywhere she goes. It isn't because she wants people to know she's wealthy (in fact, she isn't), but rather because she wants people to think she's so loved that someone would buy it for her. She has spent her entire life trying to find her own self-worth and in her mind, money spent equals love felt. It's her badge of honor. Do you want to know the saddest part? It isn't even a real diamond. The one her husband gave her wasn't good enough to make an impression on others so she took matters into her own hands.

Let's step back for a moment and think about this scenario as it relates to us. Don't get me wrong, I'm all for trying to make ourselves the best we can be. We should always strive to do whatever we can do be Godly women in every aspect of our lives. But what happens if we go about it in the wrong way? What if the Lord has given us something beautiful and we have spent years trying to make it into something we think is better?

Even if it's fake.

The strangest part of the whole thing with the girl who wore the ring is that whenever anyone complimented her on it, she smiled and thanked them, staring at it herself as if it were a beacon of acceptance. And every time that happened, I couldn't help but imagine the commentary going through her mind, knowing the truth. Obviously it doesn't matter what kind of wedding ring you wear, or if you are even married. What I want you to hear and pray about is the fact that you are created in the image of God, gifted with His love and desire to use you. Do you wear that proudly or have you stuffed it in a drawer in favor of something you think is better?

In the book of Genesis we meet a pregnant woman who is carrying twins. As she delivers them, one holds onto the heel of the other. He is born second, but it seems that from the time he enters the world he is trying to get ahead. His name is Jacob, which means "heel-grabber, usurper, deceiver."

I'm sure he wrote his mother a lovely thank-you note later in life for that.

True to his name, Jacob lives a life of deception. At one point he tricks his father into believing he is his twin brother Esau in order to steal his blessing. He succeeds, and when his brother discovers what has happened he despises Jacob and fantasizes about killing him, so Jacob flees.

Some time later (and after being a victim of deception himself!), Jacob is on the run again. This time he is traveling with his wives and children and is told that his brother Esau is coming to meet with him. He is informed that Esau has several hundred men with him. Jacob is fearful of an attack. The night before he is to see Esau, he settles his family in a safe area and then goes off on his own.

I don't think we should miss this fact, though I skimmed over it many times before I took the time to consider how important it is in my own life. It seems to me like God wanted him *alone*.

Perhaps He didn't want Jacob to be distracted by everyone else, caught up in the noise of life around him.

At this point Jacob becomes engaged in a wrestling match with the Lord, and in the process of the hours-long battle he is asked a question that will change everything, both for him and for us.

The sun starts to come up after a night of struggle and Jacob refuses to let go. It is as if he realizes this is more that a match; it could be the night that will make God the victor over much of the ugliness in his life. He refuses to let go and insists upon a blessing. At this request, the Lord simply asks him, "What is your name?"

Let's take a moment and consider the question in its truest form.

"Who are you, now?"

I've been there with the Lord.

I've wrestled until the break of dawn, begging the Lord to save me from my circumstances and bless me in spite of my transgressions. I have stared at myself in the mirror, wondering who I was underneath the makeup, underneath the mistakes, underneath the moments I wish I could do differently. I have felt shame as He asked me to say it, knowing that it was only by His grace that it would be different.

I believe in every one of those moments we have a Savior who is asking the same of us . . . *What is your name? Who have I truly intended you to be?*

This looks different for each of us but I'm willing to bet that it hit a nerve with you. Take a moment and consider your answer to the Lord's question based on what you know to be true about yourself.

Maybe you believe that your name is liar. Maybe it's untrust-worthy, unsavory, or unable. And even if nobody else knows it, you do. And in most of the interactions you have with people around you, there is a voice in the back of your mind that taunts you, *"If they only knew . . ."* Maybe that's the only way you have ever seen yourself and you can't imagine it any other way.

And this feeling is the dark of night; the dark of an enemy who wants nothing more than for you to be held prisoner here for the rest of your life. I swallow it down more than I should, this bitter pill of denial, all the while convincing myself that the charade is better than the truth.

And so we wrestle.

I love the fact that the wrestling happened through the night, where things are hard to see and equally hard to comprehend. You can't quite wrap your brain around what is happening, other than knowing you are in the fight of your life. And even though you do not know where you are getting the strength, just like Jacob, you do not let go. You fight. And suddenly, it is daybreak. The shadows disappear and the light casts awareness on the situation. We see that it is not foe we are up against, but rather the One Who came to be our ever-present help.

Who are you?

Light fills confusion, and as he looks the Lord in the face, one man answered for all of us as he answers with the only identity he'd known, *"Jacob."*

The original meaning of the word for "name" in this passage can also be translated as "reputation."

I am everything you think I am.

I am the one who tried to hold my brother back. The one who stole what should have been his. The one who took advantage of whomever I needed to in order to get ahead. The one who cheated and deceived my way into this place. I am he. Heel-grabber, usurper, deceiver.

I am she.

But his longing for a blessing from God tells us that Jacob has his mind set on tomorrow instead of yesterday. In essence, he is saying, "No matter what happens, I will not leave this fight as the same person who came to it. I will not let you go until you bless me." We are told in Hosea 12:4 that Jacob didn't just wrestle physically, but that he "wept and begged for his favor."

I know what it feels like to weep and beg for favor. What I need to get in my head is the fact that all the while I am caught up in what looks impossible, my arms are wrapped around the Possible. I don't have to be this way, Lord. I don't have to hide and I can change.

In this moment, with the reality of all he has done hanging in the air, Jacob comes face-to-face with the God who knows him. He isn't unaware of Jacob's past, and as He asks a simple question, Jacob has reached the point where he can't run anymore. He is up against a wall, backed into a corner, at the end of a long journey spent running away from himself.

Sound familiar?

So what do we do in this moment? Like Jacob, it's time we say it. We look straight to Him and tell Him everything that has followed us here. Despite the fact that He knows, He longs to hear the repentance of a heart that desires Him.

Have you wrestled with Him? Have you taken hold of His promises and refused to let go? Or have you let the fear of being known prevent you from the redemption He wants to give you in exchange?

Immediately after Jacob says his name, the Lord replies, "Your name will no longer be Jacob, but Israel . . ." (Genesis 32:28).

Israel.

Contender.

Soldier of God.

God prevails.

We are told that the Lord leaves Jacob with a limp, and forevermore he will bear it in remembrance of the One Who changed his name as the new day began.

Jacob called this place *Penial,* which means "face of God."

As I read these words I was overcome with emotion because I know that the same access to God is granted to me. I know all of the names I have had in my life, but I also know the One Who can give me a new one.

We can go to Peniel as often as we need. It may be daily, hourly, or moment-by-moment for us, but we can go meet Him face-to-face and have that which has been promised to us before Jacob ever wrestled in the night.

And He who loves us more than He despises our reputation will delight in our new name.

———

She had just touched His robe, and the crowd was breathless with anticipation. The sheer nerve of this woman, thinking she deserved something from Jesus. Who was she, anyway? Who touched Him?

He hardly let another moment pass before He blessed her with the words, "Daughter, your faith has made you well; go in peace, and be healed of your disease" (Mark 5:34 ESV).

He wasn't identifying her so that He could ridicule her or expose her shame. He was affirming her faith. Because in that moment, she believed Him to be more powerful than the condition that had crippled her for over a decade of her life. She was a woman with nothing left to lose and He recognized her faith in Him.

I imagine her weeping with relief, not just at her healing, but because she had felt something true rise up in her bones as He spoke.

He knows who I am.

We come with our infirmities and our feebleness and we beg for Him to heal us. But we fear His methods; we can't help but see ourselves as the exception to His mercy. Maybe He won't forgive me. Maybe my sin was too great. Maybe He doesn't even care. He'll just go on His way to more important things. I'm one in a crowd of millions. Who in the world do I think I am, calling out to the King?

On a dusty road leading to Nazareth, Jesus' actions answer that question.

You are the one I stop for.

You are the one I long to heal.

I know your name. I know your heart. I know everything about you, including that we would meet here today.

You are the one who sought me and I delighted in knowing your hand would reach for My hem in faith. What you saw as an act of desperation, I saw as an act of love. How many never reach out to Me at all because they don't think it would make a difference?

Now go in peace and newness of life.

Jesus makes it clear in this moment that she is not to be known as the woman with the issue of blood, but rather the woman *who had faith in Him.* She will not be known for what she was, but by what she had in spite of it.

Faith.

The same thing Jacob had shown so many years before, deep into the night as he fought his way to a different story.

Regardless of the potential for shame or hurt, neither Jacob nor the woman with the issue of blood was willing to stay who they were in light of who they could be.

Don't trade your legacy for your reputation. He is here, and He is able.

I don't want to miss that blessing either, despite how hard it is to acknowledge my sins and my weaknesses while the crowds look on. What matters in this moment is not their eyes, but His. Never mind them; just remember that they are here to witness your faithfulness to Him. They have no power over you. Go to the Lord and tell Him your name. Tell Him the depth of your brokenness and regret.

And just as dawn breaks, you will know you have been healed by the Man who gives you a new name.

You will walk for the rest of your days telling the story of redemption, not in words or deeds, but in your very existence.

Not she who would have existed if not for that night, but rather, she who chased Him in faith, and refused to let Him go.

She who rejoices in the glorious limp that reminds her of the night made day and the name that God spoke to her.

———

Lord, You know the fear that comes from a place of shame. The fear that we will be discovered and that the image we have worked so hard to maintain will come crashing down. We look in the mirror and despise the parts of ourselves that we have yet to fully surrender to You, and we fear the day when everyone will know that we have failed. It is so easy to believe that we have to keep up the charade in order to be respected, when the truth is that in our most tender, bare, and authentic state of humility is where we come the closest to Your precious hem. May we believe in You and Your love for us enough to believe that you did not create us to live a life shadowed by the feeling we are inadequate. You long for us to call out in our weakness to those who will take us by the hand, leading us until we find You. Lord, bless us with friends and family who will carve a safe place for our confessions, and will love us in a way that is worthy of You.

CHAPTER 4

MIDIAN'S HAND

FEAR OF FAILURE

Despite the meaning of his name, Gideon didn't necessarily feel like a "brave warrior."

One day he heard the voice of an angel of the Lord speak to him as he worked in his father's winepress:

> "The LORD is with you, O mighty man of valor."
> (Judges 6:12 ESV)

It seems as though Gideon misunderstood the meaning of the sentence and interpreted it as being communal statement rather than a personal one. He responded by telling the angel that it didn't seem like God was with them given the fact that they, His people, were suffering very difficult circumstances. The Israelites were being oppressively controlled by the Midianites, and Gideon believed the Lord had forsaken them.

The Lord then gave him an order: "Go in this might of yours and save Israel from the hand of Midian . . ." (Judges 6:14 ESV).

Wait. What might? Gideon certainly hasn't given us any reason to believe he thinks he is any kind of warrior. If anything he already seems defeated. And this is not the end of Gideon's doubt, nor his fear. But before Gideon could respond, the Lord asked him a question, "Do I not send you?" (6:14 ESV).

It doesn't seem like Gideon was inspired initially, as he immediately delved into all the reasons he was sure to fail. After all, he was the weakest person in his father's house and that clan was the weakest in all of Manasseh.

And the voice that said "Go" was met with fear.

———————

Years had passed since he had picked up a paintbrush.

I walked into the study of my father's home and saw his easel up, fresh canvas sitting so it faced the sunlight. His oil paints were lined up by color and the jar of dusty brushes had made its way out of a cardboard box.

"Dad?"

I heard his footsteps in the hallway as I looked at all the art books stacked up around his desk. Some had clearly been read and the others looked like they had never seen the light of day.

"Yeah, hon?" He saw what I was looking at and started nodding.

"I'm thinking I might try and pick it up again. I pulled that stuff out awhile ago but I haven't gotten too far yet." He looked at me sheepishly.

"What are you going to paint?" I surveyed the canvas and imagined the outcome. My dad is an extremely gifted painter but time had prevented him from doing it, and I was really excited to see what would come of him picking it back up.

"You know, Angela, I have a couple ideas but I've got a lot to catch up on." He motioned toward the stack of art books.

He explained that he had put the first coat of paint down just to get the canvas prepared for when he was ready to get started.

It was silent for a minute while I thought about the fact that I was very much like my father. I smiled at him and let him know I understood.

"So you're just reading about it, huh? Not really ready to do it yet?"

He shook his head.

"No, babe. I'm way too rusty. I mean, I haven't held a paintbrush in years. I need to study it first and then I'll just . . ." He trailed off as I made a face that told him I could see right through his act.

"You're scared it's not going to turn out right, aren't you?" I smiled.

"Well, you can't just pick up a brush and start painting. You won't know what you're doing and then it'll . . ."

"It'll be what, Dad?" He shifted his weight and looked me in the eye.

"Well, it would be a mess." He kept his hand on the books while I grabbed the brushes.

"You need to just do it, Dad. You're so worried about failing that you're going to read yourself right into oblivion. You're not ever going to actually do anything with all this knowledge you're gaining, so it's kind of useless, don't you think?"

So easy to say about some brushes and tubes of old paint.

Not so easy to hear as a statement about your fears.

I knew as I drove home that night that the Lord had used this moment to speak to me about my own fears of failure. I want to do it exactly right, make sure I am as fully prepared as humanly possible, and then buy (and thoroughly highlight) many more books. I want to have all the knowledge I can before I dare take a step of action.

I'm not saying it isn't valuable to learn about something before you do it, but if you have had the paint out for months and you can't tear yourself away from the manual, there's a good chance you're missing out.

I'm sure people would laugh to know that I have read virtually every book in existence on sewing, and as much as I love to sew, I think I might like learning about it even more.

When I read about it, it looks like a masterpiece in my head. When I actually construct it there are skipped stitches and the edges are uneven. It doesn't match the vision I had for it, and I feel like I have wasted the potential.

I know why the canvas sits blank; not only in his home but also in yours.

Sometimes the fear of failure steals the beauty we were meant to create.

Here's the part we need to cling to: If what we are being called to do is in God's will for us, we truly can't fail. I know it sounds like I'm making a flippant statement that should be on a poster with a guy hitting a golf ball, but what I mean is that we simply may not have the same meaning as God for the word "failure."

To me, failure means it doesn't turn out the way I wanted it to.

To God, it means I didn't pick up the brush.

Assuming that God is calling you to do something (and that isn't always easy to discern, in which case we just have to take baby steps in the direction of His voice), you will fail by being disobedient, not by a lack of success at the task.

It isn't something we like to think about because we all want to be "mighty warriors," but the Lord may use our failures for a greater cause. I know plenty of people who went headfirst into the job they were sure God had chosen for them, only to discover that they were miserable. The amazing thing is that the Lord used all of the circumstances to bring them to a deeper place of trust with Him and they chose to walk in that fullness. So maybe the success wasn't in the job working out the way they anticipated, but rather in actions that continue to obey despite the fear.

What are the things in which you fear you might fail?

Your job? Your marriage? Teaching a Sunday school class? Parenting? Being a good friend? The pursuit of holiness? You will probably notice that the things that top your list are the same things you deem have the most important outcome. That's not rocket science but it gives us some footing as we anticipate the next step.

Where do I stand to lose the most?

I fear losing the approval of those around me, so my fear of failure is most pressing in the situations that could result in people doubting me or thinking bad things about me or my motives. I will steer clear of situations where I might be made a fool and in the event that I feel embarrassed I will throw myself under the bus. I'm the first one to mock myself, as if to say, "I'm totally on your side. I think I'm weird too!"

I can't begin to count how many parties where I have stood alone, how many social interactions have led to a soaked pillow and a resolution to do it differently next time. I get really self-conscious about how much I talk and then I beat myself up because I failed as a listener. One day when I was in ninth grade someone told me I needed to be quiet and I took it very seriously. So seriously, in fact, that I decided I would use no more than one hundred words in total the next day. I sat with my mother and my little notepad at breakfast the next morning and showed her how I was going to keep a tally of all my words.

I didn't make it through first period.

I considered taping my mouth shut because I was so desperate to do the thing people wanted me to do. I blamed my mother for my verbosity, and her mother before her.

For the record, my grandmommy could talk the paint off the walls.

There is a story that has become infamous in my family when my dad was having a conversation with her while she washed dishes. He left, took a shower, and came back to the same stool he had been sitting on. She hadn't even noticed he left and was still in the middle of the same story.

Regardless of my "system" and my "plan," I failed miserably. On the third day of my word restriction program I gave up. I was never going to be the sweet, quiet girl who just nodded in the background.

I didn't know it at the time, and I still fight this part of myself every day, but I believe now that God didn't make me to be the silent girl. It isn't that one is better than the other, or that I have failed Him by being me. He never asked me to be anything other than who He made me to be, and the only failure I had was considering duct tape and carrying around a list of words with me.

That wasn't what God asked me to do.

I failed because it wasn't in His will for me to succeed at pretending.

There are certainly times when the Holy Spirit urges us to better ourselves and to seek the will of God, but our idealistic notions of what we want to happen will not necessarily be the result.

I wanted to be a different girl.

He did not.

In the event that you are curious, God will usually find a way to teach us this lesson, regardless of how we fight it.

I get a good laugh out of picturing myself as an awkward high school freshman, clinging to the image of what I thought people wanted and now seeing that the calling God had on my life was to speak.

What I saw as a character flaw, God saw as potential.

What I perceived as weakness was going to be my glory-gift.

What I was sure was failure was actually the heart of my success.

The story of Moses echoes this same sentiment, as he struggled with the idea that he was to be a mouthpiece for the Lord. He didn't see himself this way, and he wasn't really excited about trying to do something he was sure to mess up.

He begged God to reconsider, saying, "Oh my LORD, I am not eloquent, either in the past or since you have spoken to your servant, but I am slow of speech and of tongue" (Exodus 4:10 ESV).

He recognized that he was a servant of God, and yet he doubted because he knew himself and believed he also knew his lack of capacity for success when it came to speech.

God's response was in the form of a question, and it is one that has flipped my world upside-down as I consider my answer when posed with the same question.

"Who has made man's mouth? Who has makes him mute, or deaf, or seeing, or blind? Is it not I, the LORD? Now therefore go, and I will be with your mouth and teach you what you shall speak" (Exodus 4:11–12 ESV).

Well then.

Clearly God isn't a big fan of people ridiculing His masterpiece.

That doesn't mean that He isn't forgiving of our doubts and questioning; I think that's a part of life. We want to be sure we are hearing Him correctly so we ask Him to clarify in a hundred different ways.

I think there is a difference worth noting as far as the motive behind our questioning. If we are going to God with our bags packed, making sure we heard the instructions correctly, that's one thing. If, on the other hand, we refuse to even consider planning the trip and our goal is to ignore what God is telling us, that's a different story. Notice that when Moses questioned God it says that the Lord's anger kindled against Moses. Why? What angered Him? I suspect that it might have been related to the way he answered God's question and what God knew was behind his response.

God's response should have resulted in Moses showing Him respect and being willing to be molded by His Maker's hands. Moses, however, seemed determined to avoid the task.

"Oh, my LORD, please send someone else" (Exodus 4:13 ESV).

The Lord ends up sending Moses' brother Aaron with him to speak to the masses, but not before handing Moses a staff. To me, the staff represents the power God has given Moses to be a leader to the Israelites. As we know from later in Scripture, Moses is then called by God to lead His people out of Egypt, but it isn't going to go smoothly.

In fact, the Lord says to Moses, "When you go back to Egypt, see that you do before Pharoah all the miracles that I have put in your power. But I will harden his heart, so that he will not let the people go" (Exodus 4:21 ESV).

As I read this, I am struck by the fact that it seems like God is setting Moses up for failure. He's going to harden Pharoah's heart and make it so he doesn't allow them to leave, but he still wants Moses to go through the motions?

Maybe it's for the same reason He asks us to do it.

Our idea of success in this story might be if Pharoah were to become immediately speechless and agree to release the Israelites upon Moses showing Pharoah all the miraculous things God asked him to show.

In God's economy, that's not the case. It seems to me He is trying to cultivate an obedient heart in Moses, and this time, Moses complies. When Pharaoh responds the way the Lord warned Moses he would, we see Moses start to retreat again, but this time his questioning leads to a different conversation.

Moses basically asks God why He sent him to fail and accuses Him of not holding up His end of the deal.

It sounds like a pretty scathing comment given his audience, but the Lord responds by encouraging Moses to continue to fight, assuring him that His plan is intact. Exodus 6:13 tells us that God "spoke to Moses and Aaron and gave them a charge about the people of Israel" (ESV). In this passage, the original word for *charge* is *tsavah*, which means "to command."

I don't think He is angry with Moses, but rather continuing to make His will clear to him. It's as if He is saying, "You didn't fail Me. You did what I asked you to do and just because it didn't work out the way you wanted doesn't mean it surprised me. Now go get ready for what's next, because I'm not done with you."

We don't usually have the benefit Moses had in the events recorded in Exodus 6, where God revealed what would happen in the future. What we do have is a God who asks every one of us the same question when we back down from something He has called us to do.

"Who made your mouth?"

Notice that even though Moses knew beforehand that Pharaoh was going to deny his request, he still went to God with doubt. Even if He said it as clearly and directly to us as He did with Moses, we might still doubt. It's an ugly and ultimately sinful part of humanity that our impulse is often to impose our desired outcome on the plan God has for us.

This pattern continued through several instances of Moses learning what it means to truly trust and obey God. As he learns this lesson, he even manages to simultaneously fail to trust God and take credit for His power. When the Israelites begin expressing their discontent about their lack of water, God tells Moses to gather them and command of the rock for water to come forth.

However, he and Aaron gather the people around them and say, "Listen, you rebels, must we bring you water out of this rock?" (Numbers 20:10). Then, rather than calling for the water as God commanded, Moses struck the rock with his staff to bring it forth.

Not his most stellar choice.

Did the water come out of the rock? Yes.

Does that mean that Moses succeeded?

Not so much.

And as a result of him not obeying God's command to act in such a way that the power manifested would be clearly understood to have come from God, Moses is told that he will not be the one to lead the Israelites into the Promised Land.

Failure was a result of his disobedience, even though water did come forth from the rock. Again we see the correlation between God's wrath and the state of Moses' heart. He was in prideful rebellion instead of humble submission.

As I consider what God is calling me to do, despite my own misgivings, I need to remember the staff given to me.

In the midst of my fear, He hands it to me as a reminder of His great power. I am blessed in using it in exactly the way He instructs, and held accountable for the times I try to claim it as my own.

I did not create the staff, nor give it any power. I merely *hold* it, waiting for further instruction.

The only power it has is that which God Himself has given, and I did not create it any more than I created my own mouth.

Failure isn't not leading the Israelites out of Egypt the first time.

It's believing they were Moses' to lead.

It's telling God you don't want to do what He is telling you to do.

It's telling God you aren't capable of doing what He is telling you to do.

The strength that comes through carrying this precious staff is based on the humility in which I clothe it and the acceptance of a new definition of success.

Walk humbly, boldly, and gratefully in the direction you are being led, and the Lord will surely never let you fail. At least not failure as He defines it. And what other definition should matter?

While we are on the subject of failure, I think it's worth bringing up a related fear, which is the fear of success. At first this sounds silly, and maybe a category of fear that is kind of like, "fear of looking too much like a cover model," or "fear of everyone liking you." It doesn't look like something that would be a threat to us, but the truth is that there is a significant amount of research on this topic. Before I started writing this book I would have told you this might actually be a fear I didn't have. However, after I read about it and prayed through some of my decisions in life, it dawned on me that there have been plenty of times in my life where I have feared success. In turn, I have acted out of that fear.

As a friend of mine recently said, "I'm not scared of failing. I expect to fail. It doesn't take me by surprise or catch me off guard. I feel like I've gotten pretty comfortable failing, but when I succeed I can feel the panic starting. All eyes on me, and the only place I feel like I can go is down. Now that is scary."

Many of those who struggle with the fear of succeeding say they worry they will complete what they set out to, but that they won't feel satisfied when they get there. They worry that it won't live up to whatever expectations they had as far as fulfillment, joy, peace, etc. Basically it's the feeling that we might do it all and get what we thought we wanted and then be disappointed. In effect, we can self-sabotage in order to avoid this letdown.

Another side of the fear of success comes from the feeling that we don't deserve whatever it is we have been given. Let's say you have been promoted to the job you have been wanting, but as soon as you get it you start to feel guilty. You feel like the accolades should go to someone more qualified and as a result you grow uncomfortable in your own skin. It can be a fearful place to be at the top, as the experience is seldom able to live up to your expectation and rarely feels like it can continue to go well. We don't feel like we can keep up the "charade" that we are efficient, able, intelligent, gifted in whatever area we are being recognized. Because of this, there is a disconnect between the fact that we have done something successful but now we feel like we don't know how to continue being successful. Those of us who have thoughts like this may self-sabotage so we don't ever make it high enough up to be "evaluated."

Let's head back to the fear of failure for now, because I think our friend Gideon has a few lessons waiting for us, and I hope they mean as much to you as they did to me.

———

Gideon wanted to make sure he was hearing the Lord correctly, so he asked Him to confirm His will through signs. As the Lord does so, Gideon believes he is supposed to go into battle despite his lack of confidence in himself. As he is about to take his men to the battlefield, the Lord throws him another curveball, telling him to whittle his army down from 32,000 to 300 men. We see Gideon as a faithful servant, who obeyed the Lord even when it seemed unlikely he would be victorious. Even in the midst of the enemy God chose a strange combat strategy; they would not fight with weapons, but rather their voices. They were to all scream at the same time and cause the Midianites to turn on each other in the midst of the chaos.

I don't know about you but if I were going into battle, I might be tempted to have a plan B in case the screaming thing didn't pan out.

Gideon didn't show any hesitation as he obeyed what the Lord asked of him, and he won the battle.

There are five words that each of us would benefit from hearing, and one question that should shape every single war we enter. *"Do I not send you?"*

Once we are certain we have heard from the Lord, we should proceed in full confidence, even when it seems He is sending us headfirst into certain failure. I believe that God chose men like Gideon to teach us that we don't win because of our superior intellect or our incredible ability, but rather *the favor of God which rests on those who trust Him.*

If He gave us everything we needed to be successful, we would be tempted to believe it was our victory. Many times He sends us with minimum resources and directions that would make any seasoned warrior laugh. Our natural reaction when we fear failure is either to hightail it out of that situation, or perhaps more likely, to procrastinate. We don't want to admit we are completely avoiding doing something God has commanded of us (even to ourselves!), so we simply keep saying we will get to it eventually. I used to feel like I was just being lazy when I procrastinated, but the more I evaluated the situations I tended to do this in, the more I saw that it was based on a lack of faith. I don't really want to admit that I'm scared to try, so I convince myself that I just haven't done it *yet.*

When we get caught up in these thoughts, we are really not relying on God the way we should be. Instead, we're too concerned with our own abilities and we assume it isn't going to work out. Yet we can read through Scripture and see all of the times where God called someone to do something that looked impossible to the world. I love the story about all the Israelites walking around Jericho and shouting until the walls came down. It would have been really easy to say that was a ridiculous plan and move right on ahead with something more logical, but instead they were obedient and they saw the fruit of that obedience. I struggle with obeying God in these Jericho-type moments, but the times I've done so are the times when my faith felt the most real. The situations where I was the most ill-equipped were the ones that not only strengthened my faith but also the faith of those around me.

He used those times very powerfully to teach me that as long as I am listening and obedient, I will bring Him the glory.

With that said, we might read these events from the Bible and feel like we are so far removed from the people who had direct contact with God the way Moses and Gideon did. We absolutely have the same access they did, and we are fools to believe we can't ask God to reveal Himself to us and guide us according to His will. Many, many times in my life I have asked the Lord to confirm I was hearing Him correctly. I ask Him as a servant who desires to be in His will and I trust that He knows my heart when I do. In the event that I don't feel peace about a certain situation, I don't proceed. Sometimes I gain clarity later and other times I don't.

It is crucial to note that if it is something God is asking you to do, it will absolutely align with the Word of God. He will never ask you to do something that is contrary to His character or His Word, so that should be a first step when you are trying to seek His will. The best way to do this is to regularly read the Word, so you have it hidden in your heart, ready to stand up to anything you are facing.

It is so easy to begin to trust our own strength and feel like we have it all figured out. We trust ourselves more than we seek God, and this is where we normally find ourselves upside-down and hanging on for dear life. Never convince yourself that you should do something based on a "feeling" or a whim. Pray for the supernatural peace that comes from walking in step with Jesus, and then move in the direction you hear His voice calling.

One of my favorite passages about Gideon is this: "And Gideon came to the Jordan and crossed over, he and the 300 men who were with him, *exhausted yet pursuing*" (Judges 8:4, ESV, italics mine).

What are the areas in your life that you feel this fear most intensely? Do you fear you will be a failure as a spouse? As a parent? As an employee? As a friend?

Maybe you fear that you will fail at being a good Christian.

I wonder if that last one touched a nerve in you like it does in me. I think it affects all of us because we know that we are sinners and that our hearts still pull us into places we don't want to be. We struggle to get through the day feeling like we did faith "right" and we focus intently on our own missteps. I have heard several people say that their biggest fear was that they were going to slip back into the life they used to live before they were Christians and that they wouldn't be able to recover. We are all naturally sinners and the battle of the flesh is terrifically difficult to win. It's no wonder that we can get to a place where we feel like we aren't ever going to get it right. The more I convinced myself I was a "bad Christian," the more likely I was to accept my bad behavior, defending it because it lined up with what I thought of myself. More than that, I sought to maintain this image I had by wallowing in the ugliness instead of asking the Lord to help me make godly choices.

What do you believe about being a Christian? Do you think that if you don't keep every commandment of God, you are a failure? Well, I hope not, because you aren't ever going to have peace if that's your definition. I'm speaking from experience here, not from a fancy textbook, and I can tell you this: You will never "succeed" if your expectation is that you can completely overcome sin. So many of us live in fear of failing God because we see Him as perched at the edge of heaven waiting for us to make a bad choice so He can "get us." We think we are always one step away from getting banned from His presence and instead of claiming the power we have in Him to resist sin and grow in godliness, we put our heads in the ground and beg Him to give us another chance.

Have you ever worried that maybe you were running out of chances?

I'm not going to give you some trite quote about this because anything I say will pale in comparison to the truth, which is that God loves and forgives us because once we have trusted in Christ for salvation, ultimately He does not see our sin when He looks at us. He sees Jesus' perfection.

Is that hard for you to comprehend? Well then. You're in good company.

What I want to encourage you to do is to try to change the way you think of "failing" God. First of all, if you are a believer in Christ, there is nothing you can do to separate yourself from Him (Romans 8:38). You will continue to sin but you don't have to believe you are one big epic flop. Instead of spending your time lamenting your errors, pray about why those patterns of sin are present. Seek the counsel of those who have been there and ask them for advice. Tell the Lord every day that you need His help to serve Him wholeheartedly, and be disciplined in spending time in the Word. As you focus on the Bible, knowing Him more through its pages and understanding yourself more through its promises, you will more and more have the power to resist temptation.

After you have repented and committed your sin to the Lord, don't allow the enemy to tell you that you need to keep going back to it in your mind, because the more you dwell on it, the more likely you will repeat it. You will start to define yourself by your poor decisions instead of your great Redeemer, and it is far too easy to fall into old habits as the helplessness sets in. Instead, as you begin to set a pattern of repentance and submission to Him, you will see Him glorify Himself and redeem your sin.

I pray that as you work through your own fears of "failing" in your relationship with God, you will know that every person in the pew beside you (regardless of what they say) has felt the same fear. I believe it is one of Satan's most powerful tools, because if he can convince us that we are too bad to be good, we might just stop trying. Instead, look your sin in the face, repent to God, allow His Spirit to restore you to a place of peace, and begin on the path of godly choices in that area.

In each day the Lord gives us, let us become consumed with the obedient pursuit instead of the perceived victory. Let us become exhausted as we seek the face of a God who delights in giving us power through our weaknesses. Let us reevaluate failure in light of the gracious God who calls us in the same breath He called Moses and Gideon.

———

Jesus, help us to see that worldly accolades, income, the approval of others, and any other fleshly image of success pales in comparison to the success of being obedient to You. It is so easy to be caught up in the numbers, the details, the clock ticking, and all of it is for nothing if we are walking away from You. Help us not be so consumed by others, and teach us to hunger after Your will for our lives. We want to be servants who pick up the life around us and run when we hear You call. God, remind us daily that You are the only way to true success, and our failures happen only when we lose sight of this. What a gracious God to allow us to fail over and over and love us anyway . . .

CHAPTER 5

WIND AND WAVES

FEAR OF DEATH

They had been walking with Him for days, watching as He miraculously healed lepers, paralytics, and people possessed by demons. He had called each of them to follow Him, and they must have stood in awe as they saw people walk away as new creations after being in His presence. I have often wondered what their conversations were like at the end of the day when the crowds had gone home and they were alone with Him. What an amazing, unique relationship they had; not just the kind where they saw Him from afar but one where they shared life and discussed their hearts, their fears, their hopes, and their dreams.

We see glimpses of His relationships with the disciples throughout the Gospels but I love to imagine the nitty-gritty of life with the Lord. Sharing meals, laughter, and stories. These men knew Jesus of Nazareth in a way we do not and they trusted Him as a friend.

I am tempted in my own life to feel as though if I had seen Jesus face-to-face I would never doubt Him or His love for me. Yet, the truth is that even the disciples had moments of doubt and betrayal.

After a day of traveling, the Lord boards a ship with these "fishers of men" and we see a storm arise on the sea as they move from one shore to another. As the boat rocks wildly and the rain soaks them through, Jesus is found asleep, seemingly unconcerned with their safety.

I see myself in them.

People who love Him and believe that He has their best interest at heart, and yet, when the water rises and the darkness comes, we wonder if maybe He doesn't care after all.

Maybe He fell asleep and He is going to allow it to overtake us.

Maybe it was all for nothing, this faithful pilgrimage.

As the lightning flashes, they run to Him in desperation, and there on the hull of a ship that was never in danger, they cry out to the One Who controls the storm.

━━━━━━━━━

Fear of death isn't something new for me; I have had it for as long as I can remember. Every summer in my childhood included a trip to Grandmommy and Granddaddy's house in Charlotte, North Carolina. As that side of the family pronounces it, it's actually "Chaaalotte, Nawth Caalinuh." The air was thick with July's heat and we would sit on rocking chairs on the back porch while we snapped green beans and listened to stories about forever ago. It was intended to be a happy time, filled with giggling and sneaking bites of whatever was cooking. I'm sure I felt moments of that but what I remember most about those days was watching the sun fall down over Granddaddy's orchard, knowing that soon it was going to be time.

And that was an awful feeling.

We would sit in front of the TV after dinner but I can't recall a single show we watched. I remember trying to swallow my fried chicken without throwing up. And although I don't have memories of it, I have been told that on one occasion I held up two chicken legs and made them dance across the table with a clucking noise, mortifying my parents and causing Grandmommy to wipe her mouth with a clean linen towel and clear her throat in the way that meant *"Well I'll be . . ."*

During the day I would wander into the guest room I slept in with my sister and practice getting in the big bed. I would close my eyes and pretend it was the middle of the night. I usually couldn't do it for too long and I would get up and make my way over to the little dresser that still had my mother's things on it from many years ago. I'd look in the tiny hand mirror, hair set in pink spongy curlers, pursing my lips and shaking my head while whispering, "Don't be afraid. There's nothing to be afraid of" while putting on waxy red lipstick.

There was a crystal bottle of old perfume that sat in the room that was meant to be decoration, but on a rainy afternoon I decided it would be my coat of armor. I squeezed the little pump and closed my eyes, positive I had found the trick. Although it didn't shake the fear from me, it did give me a powdery distraction for a few minutes while I combed my hair. Then it was off to the next "cure."

I would sit on Granddaddy's lap and ask him question after question until he would shush me, because I thought for sure if I could make him talk I wouldn't have to go to bed. Eventually it was time, and while the smell of leftover dinner floated through the air and Grandmommy rinsed dishes, I was sent to my room for the night.

I hated that room.

It smelled like mothballs and the sadness of my mother's childhood.

I would lie as still as I could and try to listen to the grown-ups talk because as long as they were awake everything was all right. They were on the lookout for any kind of trouble and they would protect me from burglars and darkness. I would typically not make it in the room more than a few minutes before the sound of my own heart would scare me enough to jump up and slide on my belly down the hallway, guided by flashes from the TV in the other room.

I would make my way to the edge closest to my family and sit up against the wall for support, listening to the sound of life, reminding myself there was nobody in the backyard, nobody trying to come through the window, nobody who wanted to hurt my family. Occasionally, I would get away with sitting there for a few minutes, but then I would accidentally make a sound and get sent back down the hallway.

One summer I came up with an elaborate plan to have my younger sister Jennifer keep "watch" over our room. It was simple; we would sleep in shifts. I would set the alarm for every two hours and when it went off we would trade. That way, we each got a couple of hours of sleep and we were guaranteed to be safe. On the first night of the new plan, I awoke to my sister snoring with a book in her hands and light shining on her face. I threw a stuffed dog at her and reminded her of the consequences for no one being on duty. I'm sure I made up some terrible story and promised her a reward I couldn't even give her; but, it worked.

Well, it worked for a few nights.

Then she decided if it was her time to die, she was just going to accept it. She told me she wasn't scared of night like I was. She rolled over in her bed defiantly and I stared at the ceiling with one thought going through my mind. A thought that has rattled around my head many, many times since then.

"Now it's all up to *me*."

Under the flowery sheets I would breathe in and out while I listened to the cicadas and tried to pretend it was morning. The weight of responsibility was unbearable and I had to poke my sweaty little face out from under the covers occasionally so I could catch my breath.

The rooms have changed. The story has changed. The days are different now, but not entirely.

As I rock my daughter to sleep tonight, I'll remember the sound of the creaking as we rocked our summers away on the porch and I will dread the moment where I have to lay her down in her crib. I will climb in my bed, heart pounding, while I do what I've done for more than thirty years

Pretend it's morning.

As someone who likes to consider things logically, I have occasionally been able to convince myself that the odds are against something happening to me or someone close to me. That worked for a while too.

At least, until January 7, 2008, when I walked into a room that would push me so far into the depths of pain that I felt I might not ever recover.

I was pregnant with my fourth daughter, and the ultrasound was a formality. I was going to see her scoot around and watch her heart beating. The odds said that this was going to be a normal appointment, but it didn't turn out that way.

I walked out an hour and a half later in complete shock, trying to process the fact that I had been told my daughter would not survive. Every fear I had pushed to the back of my mind to instead comfort myself with statistics was suddenly my reality. The seal had been broken, and I was terrified. How could I survive this? Who did God think He had chosen for such tragedy? I wasn't one of the strong ones who could handle this burden. He knew that, and yet, here I was pregnant with Audrey and face- to-face with death.

In the months that followed, Todd and I chose her burial plot, planned her funeral, and I cried until my eyes were swollen shut. I pleaded for God to save her and I did everything I could to just make it through each day in one piece. I know people thought I was brave but I knew the truth: I was terrified and I was weak.

It was a daily battle as the day of her birth neared. I was often overcome with imagining what was going to happen. She might gasp for air or be in pain; she might not even live to meet us. It was a dark time for our family as we marked the calendar with the day she would come into the world and likely leave it as well. April 7, 2008.

She lived for two and a half hours and she showed me a place in my heart I had never seen before; God blessed me with a peace that cannot be explained. When she went to be with the Lord, there was no fear in the room. It was quiet, precious, and difficult beyond words—but I wasn't afraid. I held her body long after she was gone and I stared into the depths of my greatest fear.

The following month I lost my three-month-old nephew to SIDS.

I knew something was wrong when the phone rang late in the night but I tried to ignore my thoughts. When I knew he was gone I fell to the ground in despair, hardly able to comprehend that it was happening again.

I cannot forget the images of him and the deep sorrow that accompanied a life that felt unfinished. How do you go on believing in a God that allows such a thing happen? How do you trust that He is watching and in control when you have to fold the tiny clothes of a baby that didn't live to wear them? Who is this God Who sleeps while the waves threaten the boat?

I found myself onboard with these fishers of men, watching as the sky grew dark and the water rose. *Where was He?*

Fundamentally I could have told you that I believed in Him and that I trusted Him with my life, but I think that until this point in my life I did a much better job of believing it for other people than I did for myself.

The worst was upon me. The thing I had dreaded for years was a reality. There were two people I loved buried deep within the earth, side by side and never to be held here again.

In some sense, I felt like He had taken His hands off the wheel and all of life was fair game for disaster. Even then I knew this was the voice of the enemy but it was incredibly difficult to move past.

I will never forget the vacation we took to the beach shortly after we lost our daughter. I was numb, clinging to any semblance of normalcy I could get my arms around, and my family thought it would be a good idea to get away.

Belly still swollen from delivery, I sat on the hot sand and stared at the miles of people around me. I was consumed with how they acted so calm. They read books, built sandcastles, laughed at the waves, and snacked on chips while the sun shined on their children. I was beside myself with fear. I felt like I was an extra on a movie set.

Don't they know they are all going to die? How are they acting so normal? They don't know how or when, and they are going to die. Every single one of them. It might be on the way home or fifty years from now. It might be cancer, a car accident, a fluke, an aneurism, an illness, a drowning . . .

My hands were shaking as I stood up and walked to the edge of the water. I listened to the sound of the waves crashing and I begged God to give me peace as the fear came over me. I remember my teeth chattering as I allowed my mind to drift to all kinds of worst-case scenarios,. After several minutes I looked up in search of my family. They were nearby, Popsicles dripping on their bathing suits without a care in the world. I was frantic with worry and I couldn't seem to slow it down in my mind. All the possibilities, all the things that might happen, and me, with my hands tied in all of it.

I didn't want them to see me crying so I started to walk down the beach as I talked to the Lord. I would love to say that this was the only moment I can remember where I was paralyzed by the fear of death, but it wasn't.

At its core, it is the recognition that I do not have control of life. God Himself knows my last day on this earth and how it is that I will be brought to Him. It isn't for me to know. As with so many other fears, the struggle is in the acknowledgement that no matter how long I spend worrying about it, I won't be any closer to an answer.

I say I have a fear of flying, but really I think I'm just afraid to die.

They are five words I have long swallowed because I didn't want to seem different or unspiritual . . . *I am afraid of death.*

News of crime scenes, murders, and accidents are magnetic to me in a way I despise. I am so terrified that I can't bear to look away. Then in the middle of the night I convince myself that I hear something outside my window and I imagine what could happen next. I am embarrassed to write this because it doesn't seem very noble, nor does it honor the Lord the way I want to honor Him with my thoughts. But I am praying that someone reading will be nodding her head, acknowledging that even those of us who believe in heaven fear our departure from the world.

I have read stories of incredible missionaries who have been martyred for their faith and I can't help but wonder if I would have that kind of selfless courage. I want to believe I would but sometimes the fear clouds my love for the Lord. I know I'm not alone in this fear, but I think that Christians have a hard time talking about it, which just makes us feel more like outsiders. I mean, to be absent from this body is to be present with the Lord Himself. What kind of Christian wouldn't want that, right?

On that particular trip to the beach I spent a lot of time praying and asking the Lord to replace my thoughts with faith. One night I saw my grandmother out on the balcony by herself and I snuck out to talk to her.

"Grandma, can I ask you a really weird question?" She nodded and adjusted her hearing aid. That thing never stops buzzing and it drives her crazy. I think she hears better without it, but just like the little medicine holder she has filled with her daily vitamins, she does things she thinks are age-appropriate at ninety-two. She doesn't want to feel like the kid at the party with the wrong shoes, you know? So she wears the hearing aid and carries the pill-pack with the weekdays on it like all the other ninety-something-year-olds at the Y.

"Are you ever afraid of dying?"

She smiled a little and shook her head from side to side.

She wasn't.

I asked her why and she told me that she had lived a beautiful life and it just didn't scare her. I stared at her in amazement because I wanted her faith. I wanted the freedom that came from not having to obsess about what might or might not happen.

I wanted to look at the ocean like it was beautiful and not something that could swallow me up.

This was a particularly hard season for me, having been to three funerals in the past several weeks. The enemy taunted me with images of something happening to me, my husband, or my children and I have to admit that I allowed him to do so.

I felt like a failure as a Christian. I was in a position of encouragement to others and I felt like this was a weakness that made me less than I should be. I prayed, I read Scripture, I asked the Lord to help me, and yet, I still layed awake at night in tears of desperation. All I could think about was that I couldn't survive the loss of another loved one. I can only describe this feeling as torment. It nearly consumed me. I was ashamed at what I perceived as a lack of faith. Even now, more than two years later, I am choked up as I remember these moments.

What I long to do is to wrap this up with a beautiful bow and tell you that the Lord has removed this fear from my life. Sadly, that isn't the case. I still struggle with this fear. However, I now see it a little differently than I once did. I want to share that with you in the event that it might encourage you.

I think it's natural for us to fear death—both our own and the death of those we love. It is a horrific reality that sin exists. Satan delights in our sleepless nights and our doubts in God's sovereignty. We must continually turn it over to the Lord and surround ourselves with people who urge us to trust His goodness. On a practical level, I think there are things in our lives that give the enemy a foothold and each of us needs to identify what those are.

Have you ever noticed that your fears have a magnetic quality? For example, I had to limit the amount of time I spent watching the news and reading tragic stories online. I receive many e-mails from people who have suffered loss but I have come to realize that by immersing myself in their stories I add to my own fears. I pray there comes a day when that isn't the case, but for now, I have set up some different boundaries that help me tremendously. I have fear, yes, but I don't allow myself to be in situations where I feel like the enemy is rejoicing in that fear.

Let me give you an example of what I would call a healthy fear in this area: I am afraid to run around by myself in the park in the middle of the night. Well, that's probably a wise choice, don't you think? I can listen to the rational side of fear but stop short at obsessing about the possible scenarios. I can have reasonable, healthy guidelines for avoiding danger but that doesn't mean I let myself get lost in the possibilities. Each person has to flesh this out in his or her own life. Ask the Lord for guidance. When you realize you are dwelling on the fears, turn instead to the Bible.

I am amazed at how many women I have talked to who say they have the same struggles. Like every other fear, Satan clings to the thought that we will be ashamed to tell others. Once I opened up to some women I trusted about this fear, I felt such great relief through their understanding and suggestions.

Fearing death is a part of life, and because we "do not have a high priest who is unable to sympathize with our weaknesses" (Hebrews 4:15), we should feel safe going to Him with our concerns.

As Matthew Henry so eloquently explains, there is but one solution to this fear.

> Let those who dread death, and strive to get the better of their terrors, no longer attempt to outbrave or to stifle them, no longer grow careless or wicked through despair. Let them not expect help from the world, or human devices; but let them seek pardon, peace, grace, and a lively hope of heaven, by faith in Him who died and rose again, that thus they may rise above the fear of death.[2]

David, who was called a "man after God's own heart," experienced the fear of death as his best friend-turned-enemy sought to kill him. In Psalm 55 he says, "My heart is in anguish within me; the terrors of death assail me. Fear and trembling have beset me; horror has overwhelmed me" (vv. 4–5).

Many times, like David, I have dreamed about what it would be like to flee from the storm to a safe place only to be reminded that the Lord is our refuge. He is the safe place I have spent so many days trying to create for myself. Later in this psalm, David urges us to cast our cares on the Lord, reminding us that He is trustworthy even as he anticipates the enemy.

It gives me peace to know that the Lord has given us examples in His Word of people who were faithful, devoted servants of Christ who had fear. What these examples teach us is that we have an opportunity to glorify God in how we respond to fear. As he wrote the end of Psalm 55, David was still unsure of his future, and yet he turned his fear into an opportunity to trust. What a beautiful image of belief and peace in a moment that could have destroyed him.

―――――――――

I am comforted in the knowledge that Jesus understands, and more than that, He came in order to "free those who all their lives were held in slavery by their fear of death" (Hebrews 2:15).

This brings up an interesting question. Scholars disagree as to whether or not Jesus Christ felt fear of death. We are told in Luke 22 that Jesus asks His heavenly Father to let the cup pass Him if God would will it, and then we see Him in anguish as He considers His future. It is not entirely clear to me if Jesus was grieving the separation He knew He was going to have with God the Father or if there was also a human fear of death. We aren't told specifically that the Lord felt fear, but we do know that His experiences on earth were sufficient for Him to be able to identify with every suffering and temptation we experience—including our fear of death (Hebrews 2:17–18; 1 Corinthians 10:13). Whether or not Jesus experienced the fear of death in the way that we experience it, we do sense a great agony as Jesus anticipates the next part of His Father's plan. In His own words, He is "overwhelmed with sorrow to the point of death" (Matthew 26:38).

At this point, Jesus did two significant things. First, He requested the fellowship of His disciples. Second, He spent time alone in prayer. We do not know His precise motives for including the disciples, but scholars believe His motives included ensuring

His disciples would see and hear His prayer and that they would be near during this crucial time of God's plan. We should find encouragement in His example. The comfort we experience with other believers is a powerful balm for our fear and we should remember that our dependence on the Lord in such times is a significant testimony. Our relationship with others is a significant factor in overcoming the fear of death.

In fact, I asked hundreds of women what they feared most in life and many said "dying alone." It wasn't just the fear of being gone, or suffering in the last moments of life, but the fear of not having someone close enough in spirit to "keep watch" with them. Jesus was, in essence, asking them to empathize with Him as the hour of His death loomed just ahead. His desire was to have communion with His Father and for His disciples to be near as He did.

As much as the disciples loved Jesus, they could not keep their eyes open despite His many requests. Even in this very subtle way we are reminded that people will never be able to live up to our expectations and our desires in every moment. Just as Jesus did, we must remain in communion with God, asking Him to bring us peace in the face of calamity.

―――――――

I was so concerned about Abby and Ellie after we lost Audrey. Kate was too young to really comprehend it but the twins were very sensitive and at an age where they were easily frightened. I had explained to them that she was going to die, and that her body would be like a doll but her spirit would be in heaven with God. Even though I had told them it wasn't something that we needed to fear, I prayed that God wouldn't allow them to be impacted in a way that would terrify them or haunt them in years to come. They handled everything really well with Audrey, but when we found out that their cousin Luke had passed away, they started to be very fearful that something was going to happen to one of us.

In truth, we felt the same way. We drove to Georgia to be with my brother and sister-in-law as they coped with the staggering loss of their son. All the way there I jumped as cars switched lanes and traffic lurched. When we arrived, all the kids were in the swimming pool and the tension was palpable as each parent continually called out their children's names to make sure they were doing okay in the water. As dusk fell and the children giggled and swam, too young to comprehend the loss the way we did, my brother-in-law, Greg and I stood at the edge of the water. We stared at them, bouncing in and out of their inner tubes, goggle-eyed, and hoarse from playing. It seemed ridiculous that they were so unaware of the gaping loss, and yet it occurred to me that they had something we didn't.

Greg's eyes were swollen and red and his arms hung lifelessly at his sides while he stared at them. "I mean look at them, Angie. Just playing and having a great time like none of this happened. Can you imagine?"

"Truth be told, Greg, if we could really comprehend where Luke and Audrey are right now, we would be filled with the same joy." He nodded and we both watched as they splashed and kicked their way into a good night's rest.

What a beautiful way to live life; without the knowledge that we could lose it all.

While I believe all of this on paper, it is a very difficult thing to live out. To truly believe with everything in me as the Bible says, that death is sweeter than life, would revolutionize the way I live and love. It would constantly remind me that the worst isn't as bad as it seems because He is on the other side of it. As I mentioned earlier, I say I am afraid of flying, but really, it isn't the plane I fear. There isn't anything inherently scary about a chunk of metal. What is scary to me is the thought that *it might not stay in the air.* When it starts to get bumpy I scan the seats to see if anyone else is terrified. Usually they aren't, and it helps to reassure me that this is normal. The fact that we hit a rough patch doesn't mean we are going down.

That's not just true for airplanes, you know.

Where are your rough patches? Letting your teenage daughter drive to a party on the other side of town? What about seeing your husband receive chemotherapy? Can you honestly say you never fear that the call in the middle of the night won't bring you news that something has gone terribly wrong? Most of our common fears are actually heightened responses to what we perceive threatens our life. It might be dogs, or water, or even spiders, or small places. They all carry with them the feeling that we might not be able to escape, and that feeling is like a noose around the neck, day in and day out.

We struggle to gain control and we struggle even more to let it go. How beautiful would it be to truly believe without question that we were only in the prelude?

I don't believe God wants us to go through life with a fear of what our afterlife will look like, but He knows that the idea of eternity is impossible for us to comprehend. This can make us uneasy and I believe it is yet another opportunity to believe in spite of tangible evidence. We choose to believe in heaven the same way we believe in God when the phone rings in the middle of the night or the plane bumps in the sky. Not because we can explain it in our humanity, but rather because we trust in His divinity.

I have walked through the valley of the shadow of death, and I imagine you have as well. There is great sadness in the valley, and there is confusion, but I can say with certainty that I trust Him more than I did before having and losing Audrey. It isn't always easy to love a God who you can't see or touch, but when

I read Scripture and spend time with Him in prayer, I am reminded of His goodness. I trust that which I cannot see or understand—and those are the moments when I feel the most alive.

———

Several years ago I got to experience something that forever changed my view of fear.

We were out of town with my side of the family and were taking a shopping trip before dinner. We walked past a giant jumpy ride that looked like torture to me but the kids thought it might be fun so we got in line. It was ridiculously expensive, which I wasn't concerned about because I knew they would never in a million years actually do it. They were terrified of anything that even remotely looked dangerous, and this getup involved being harnessed into a safety seat and then flung as high as the trampoline and bungee cords would let you jump.

And it was high.

We rounded the first corner and as a little boy flew up into the air I waited for them to tell me they had changed their minds. But they didn't. They just watched and continued through the line. As we made it to the final approach I looked at Todd as if to say, "What is happening here?" I mean, I wanted to support them doing something new but this was crazy. I didn't want to freak them out because I try not to pull them into my fears, so I just encouraged them as they went. We paid our money and I asked who would go first. Abby volunteered meekly, looking back at me to see if I was okay with it.

"Yay, Abby! It is going to be SO much fun!" I wish we had it on video because I rocked the fake confidence voice. I really didn't think she was going to let them strap her in. She did. And then she jumped as hard as she could while smiling at us the whole time.

You could have knocked me over with a feather.

Next up was Ellie, who is probably my most fearful child. She takes after me so much, always wanting to gather information and feel like she knows what's coming next in every possible second. She considers every choice as though her life depends on it, which breaks my heart because she inevitably feels like she made the wrong decision no matter what she does. I bent down and gave her the money to hand to the lady working the ride. She looked at me and I could see she was starting to panic, so I did my best to reassure her.

"Honey, Abby just did it and she had a great time. If we leave I think you're going to be bummed you didn't do it."

She looked at Abby, who was giving her a high five as she walked back over.

"It's awesome, Ellie. You can see the whole place from up there!"

Ellie started to shake her head like she wasn't going to do it.

I pretended like I didn't notice and gave her a nudge to move ahead.

"Is it okay, Mommy? I mean, is it really okay?" she asked.

"Of course it's okay, babe. I'll wait right here and watch you jump. Go ahead." Todd nodded with me and she finally handed over the sweaty stack of dollar bills and made her way to the platform area.

She reached the spot where she would get strapped in and I saw her face crumble. She hung her head, lifted her shoulders, and squeezed her little eyes shut. I was pretty sure we were about to get a refund and I started to motion to the man to send her back.

Just before he did, she did something I couldn't believe.

She opened her eyes, stepped back, and waited for him to buckle her up.

I looked at Todd, who was yelling words of encouragement with Abby right beside him doing the same. Ellie cracked a tiny, scared smile as they finished up the round of affirmation.

The man who buckled her in said something to her and she nodded. As soon as she did, he released her into the air.

I held my breath, poised to yell for them to let her down. On her first bounce she opened her eyes really wide and held her body stiffly as she came back down, but by the third bounce she had loosened her grip and looked like she might be enjoying herself. All the people standing around had seen her almost back out so they began yelling along with us.

I'm not sure she heard a single sound.

At one point she jumped as hard as her legs would let her and she soared up into the sky like she didn't have a care in the world. As she reached the peak of the jump, she threw her head back, with her eyes closed and an ecstatic smile spread from one side of her face to the other. I snapped the camera at that precise moment, with her toes pointed in midair, enjoying the experience she almost missed because of fear.

Even then, as I studied my camera, I felt the Lord telling me to look closely at her face.

Trust Me, daughter. I have beautiful things in store for you . . .

That photograph is a constant reminder to me when I am faced with an obstacle that feels impossible, a fear that seems bigger than life.

I don't want to miss it, Lord . . .

In this life, we are always at the edge of the pool, a few years beyond believing that life is always good and fair. We know better, and as a result we can feel swallowed by the uncertainty. I decided during that time at the side of the pool with my brother-in-law that I want to live my life like the kids were on that hot Georgia day. God knows when our days will end and He knows the restless fear of our hearts. The best and most glory-giving thing we can do is to love the water while we have it, always mindful that there is a greater place awaiting us.

The storm had reached a fevered pitch. As the waves crashed over the edge of the boat, the disciples became panicked. Didn't He care? Wasn't He going to save them? How could He sleep through the storm, knowing that they were all going to die?

We learn a great lesson by considering how Jesus lounged on the ship. Those around Him knew He could perform miracles, but when it came down to trusting in miracles for their own lives, the trust wavered. I see this more in my life; if someone is ill or fearful, I am the first one to encourage them to have faith. But if it is me, I tend to believe He has fallen asleep.

At the heart of my fear is the burning question of whether or not I really matter to Him the way I want to believe I do.

Several years ago we were on a boat and my daughter Ellie befriended a woman who had been diagnosed with a terminal form of cancer. Standing in between this woman and Todd's dad, as the woman's scarf blew in the wind, Ellie started asking her questions about why she was wearing it. The woman explained that she had been getting treatment that made her hair fall out, but she still wanted to feel pretty so she chose a scarf that matched her outfit every day. Ellie asked her if she was getting better and the woman told her that she was praying she would, but she wasn't sure.

I watched as Ellie processed this, and even though I couldn't hear all of the conversation, I was worried about her response. She surprised me as she looked out over the water and pointed into the distance.

"See that?" She motioned toward the waves and the woman nodded.

"Those waves were made by God. He also made that sand, and that bird, and this boat. He makes the sun come up and go down and He has a lot of power." The woman smiled at Ellie, listening intently.

"His hands are so big," she continued, "that He can do all of these amazing things." Ellie paused to consider something that seemed to trouble her.

"But I think they are too big for Him to make a peanut butter and jelly sandwich."

I heard my father-in-law burst out laughing and he later relayed the conversation back to me. The woman in the scarf thought it was equally funny, and Ellie was very pleased that she had said something that made everyone happy.

Later that night I laid in my bed while the cruise ship sailed through the darkness. The weather was making the waves a little choppy and I felt nervous about being onboard. The little cruise channel on our TV was giving updates and saying it was probably going to get worse before it got better. I felt my heart beating out of my chest and my hands were sweating through my pillowcase as I held onto it for dear life.

I thought about what Ellie had said to the woman earlier in the day and I smiled as I realized that this was one of the reasons that I feared. I don't doubt that God created the heavens and the earth, nor do I doubt that He raised men from the dead and sits at the right hand of the Father. These are all big things for a big God.

But I am little in the hand of a big God and I fear He will not be able to make His fingers small enough to hold onto me.

I know it isn't biblical, but I often feel like I might slip off His radar. It's as if I believe that He might be busy with something more important and then look up and *poof*, my plane has crashed. My boat has sunk. My little girl didn't see the car coming. My husband got a call from the doctor saying it's worse than we thought it would be. It's all falling apart and He is just too BIG to notice.

It looks sillier on paper than it feels in life.

Perhaps you struggle with *feeling* like your life really matters to God the way you *intellectually* know it does. Maybe you believe His promises to other people, but when you are being thrown around in the waves you feel like maybe He's just resting up for something more pressing.

Me too.

Fortunately, we are both wrong.

Jesus does calm the storm, but He also poses a question to His disciples. This question falls squarely on our shoulders as we experience the same fear they did.

"Where is your faith?" (Luke 8:25).

Is it in the structure of the boat? The wood that was used to shape it? Is your faith in the other disciples? What about your job? Your health? Your navigation system, your doctor, your vitamins, your treadmill, your genes?

Have you convinced yourself that something you can control is controlling you?

Then you will surely be disappointed.

Remember when Jesus first called the disciples? Four of them were fishermen, and after a particularly unsuccessful day on the water, the Lord gave Simon a strange order. He told him to "put out into deep water, and let down the nets for a catch" (Luke 5:4).

Simon kindly explained that he had been out all night trying to get fish to no avail, but then he said he would put down his nets because the Lord had told him to.

I love that.

I've been trying in my own strength, Lord. And I have nothing to show for it. But I trust You, so if You tell me to do it again I will. He might not have believed the outcome would be any different but he still obeyed. As Jesus promised, Simon and the sons of Zebedee end their day with more fish than their nets can hold.

The men fall before the Lord professing their iniquity in light of who He is, and He responds, "Don't be afraid; from now on you will catch men" (Luke 5:10).

In order to see the miracle, you have to put your faith in the One Who tells you to go out into the deep. And when the sky grows dark with rain and the water starts pouring in, remember the day He told you to do it anyway.

I long to be a fisher of men, one who trusts in the Lord of the broken nets. As I cast my line, so I cast my cares on He who will sustain me (Psalm 55:22).

I wonder if the disciples realized in that moment what the Lord wants all of us to know in our fear.

He didn't just come for the lepers and the blind men.

He came for you.

What Jesus did so many years ago in the garden of Gethsemane is what I need to do today. I will gather people I trust and I will rely on the God who holds the cup.

When it is my turn to drink, I pray I will do as the Lord did and lay down my life for the One Who stilled the waves; the One Who sent me out into the deep so I could love Him more than I feared the night.

━━━━━━━━━

God, we don't want to live lives in fear of what is to come. We don't want to taint whatever You have for us as we react out of our humanity. Remind each person reading these words that You are trustworthy and that death has no sting in light of all that You have promised. Don't let us miss the beauty that can grow in the shadow of fear as we turn our eyes to You instead of the world. We will give You all the glory, Lord.

CHAPTER 6

THE FIRST STONE

FEAR OF MY PAST CATCHING UP TO ME

Her story is one of my favorites in all of the Bible because it gives me hope.[3]

While I am not an adulterer, I see a lot of myself in her. Her eyes scanned the crowd and she listened as the men revealed the ugliness of her sins. They thrust her out in front of the masses, detailing her indiscretion for all to hear. There is no record that she put up any fight or protest, and we are left to assume that she is guilty of the charges of adultery.

Surely she knew what was going to come of her as she looked at Jesus as He stood with them, watching every move. The law said that she should be stoned, and I imagine she braced herself for the punishment of death. It wouldn't be a quick, painless death, either. She would suffer through the physical pain and the emotional torture that she knew she deserved. I can imagine they were screaming at her, accusing her, consumed with the anger they had for what she had done.

Out of the chaos came movement.

One by one, the crowd turned their attention from her to Him, and our Lord did something compelling. Instead of giving the woman what she deserves, He didn't say a word.

What He did could be considered one of the most provocative moments recorded in the Bible.

He knelt down and began to draw on the ground with His finger. He didn't look up at the others and was focused on what He was writing. It is the only incident in the Bible where we see Jesus writing. As I read the words I find myself leaning closer to Him, studying His work.

There, in the ground is the answer I have feared my entire life.

My stomach turns as I consider what He might say about who I really am, and I imagine she wondered as well. I am guilty as charged. No defense. Just me, the crowd that waits, and the God who knows it all.

As His hand moves, we all have the same question burning in our minds.

Lord Jesus, what do You say to a sinner like me?

―――――――

It has been more than ten years since I joined my first Bible study. I was a graduate student at Vanderbilt University and I was at a major crossroads in my life. For years I had felt like I was flailing, recognizing all the poor choices I had made and the repercussions that still haunted me.

A friend of mine asked me to go with her to a Bible study and I had no idea what that was. I was lonely and it was right down the street so I agreed to come. She told me I needed to get the study workbook and told me about a store downtown that should have it.

I skipped my afternoon class and headed to the store, but I didn't make it in the first time I tried. I sat in the parking lot talking on my phone and after evaluating the window displays I decided this was a bad idea.

These people were perfect.

Perfect makeup, perfect smiles, perfect faith.

And I was the class-skipper listening to the Beastie Boys in my car.

I drove back home, called my friend and told her my schedule was busier than I realized and that I wasn't going to be able to commit to Monday nights. I told her I would go once to meet her friends, but I wasn't going to buy the book, and I also wasn't ever going back to the store with the 4,000 Jesus eyes looking at me.

Monday rolled around and I tried to find a conservative (ugly) outfit to wear. I fixed my hair and makeup and met her outside, lamenting that this was sure to be a train wreck. For some reason I still remember getting in the elevator with my friend Audra and seeing a sign that had been posted. Evidently someone had been in a hurry and had typed "STAY CLAM" instead of "STAY CALM." We got a terrible case of the giggles and to this day we say that to each other when things get crazy.

As soon as the apartment door opened I felt like I was going to be sick. I shook hands with everyone and excused myself to the bathroom so I could breathe. A few minutes later everyone whipped out their giant Bibles and like a choreographed routine they all landed on the same page. I looked at Audra, eyes crunched, rebuking her for not telling me I would need a Bible.

Because, you know, the term "Bible study" was a little ambiguous.

I'm pretty sure I fumbled in my purse like a big Bible might fall out and then explained that I must have forgotten it at home.

The leader of the group asked us to go around in a circle and introduce ourselves and I started sweating like I was on trial. I wracked my brain for something normal that would satisfy these alien-girls who were obviously unaware of what I had been doing the weekend before.

My turn came and I rubbed my hands together and told them that I was happy to be there (a lie), that I had left my Bible at home (lie #2), and that I hadn't had a chance to get the Bible study book yet (well at least I'm consistent). The sweet girl leading just smiled at me like I was a puppy and said, "Well . . . good news! I have TONS of Bibles and I went ahead and got you a copy of the study!" She was giddy as she handed them to me and I did my best to pretend this didn't feel like torture. I didn't want to get their hopes up about me because they were bound to find out I wasn't one of them.

"I really appreciate that. You all seem so kind and I would love to hear more about God but my only experience with Him was when my mom gave me a bowl haircut and I prayed it would grow out by morning. It didn't, and I haven't really been that impressed with Him since then." I squeezed my lips together to smooth my ChapStick, shrugging my shoulders. Nobody smiled. That should do the trick. I looked at the girl next to me and passed the imaginary "your turn" baton.

She wasn't ready for me to be done, as evidenced by the fact that she was looking at me like I was a combination of road kill and "bless your heart" all rolled up in one.

"I'm just kidding." I smiled. "I mean, I really did pray about my hair when I was 6, but I don't hate God or anything. I mean, I don't really know enough about Him to hate Him. And I haven't ever been to a study like this and I'm a little confused about . . ." I trailed off when I saw Audra doing the fake chop motion to her neck.

"Anyway, thank you for the book. It looks like fun." This

time I threw the invisible baton and did the official head-nod to clarify it was really time to move on.

I stared at the next girl to speak, feeling my face flush with humiliation. I looked down and started flipping through the "Breaking Free" study that Miss Happy-Pants had gifted me.

I looked up at Audra, fighting tears. She smiled at me and I saw her mouth two words while the chatter continued.

"*Stay. Clam.*"

The following week I came more prepared. I had my Precious Moments Bible and I had completed my assignment. It had taken me four hours total because I didn't know where any of the books of the Bible were (in fact, I didn't know they were called "books of the Bible"). Well it turns out we were going to revisit all of them, so I kept flipping to the index and trying to catch up while everyone else practiced synchronized verse-finding.

One of the girls noticed I was struggling and told me that the woman who wrote the study was notorious for moving around in her Bible really fast. She said she even had a hard time finding the pages sometimes, which made me feel better because she had crosses on her earrings and her pendant.

She had three crosses on her person, for crying out loud. That had to count for something, right?

She showed me that her Bible had little tabs saying the name of the books. Brilliant. I was going to have to get some of those. Which probably meant I was going to have to go in the Jesus store.

I noticed mine had more books in it than theirs and they explained that it was because mine was a Catholic Bible. Later that night I called my dad and told him I had the most books in my Bible of the entire group.

I think he was really proud of that accomplishment.

I have to imagine that God thoroughly enjoyed watching me be loved and accepted by a group of people to whom I felt so diametrically opposed. Eventually I braved the store and purchased a new Bible designed for women along with a set of colorful tabs. The girls in study delighted in my passion for learning and made a point of cheering me on as I flipped through the pages. They had no idea that on Sunday nights I practiced finding the references so that I could impress them.

I began to forgive God for the bowl-cut fiasco and my heart grew fond of Him through study. Several weeks later I had a dear woman sit down with me and address some of the patterns she was seeing in my life. I started breathing quickly and felt my eyes sting as I told her I didn't think I was going to be the person she was hoping I would be. She was kind but convincing, and as I did my assignments for the next several weeks I began to feel like there might be something to this Jesus who promised to be with me. My boyfriend at the time wouldn't even promise that. I mean, who in the world thinks I am worth staying with?

I loved to watch Beth Moore on the videos. It was my favorite part of the study because she made me feel like my past wasn't going to swallow me up. She was pretty honest, saying she had made some bad choices herself, and it made me want to love God the way she did. It also made me want to shop for cute jeans, but that is another matter entirely.

It wasn't until months later that I would sit in my car on a rainy night in Nashville, crying until I couldn't see.

I knew He was real and I knew I needed to confess my sins and invite Him into my life. I will never forget the smell of fresh rain and the way I fell so hard for Him.

The shame-lifter, the God-made-man, the burden-carrier, the lover of my soul . . . the One Who waited for January 17, 2000 the way only a Father could; with forgiveness and grace like I had never known.

As I write these words my eyes are swimming in tears because I remember that moment like it just happened. I knew everything

I was, everything I had done, everywhere I had gone, and yet He whispered, *"It could never be farther, now . . ."*

But I couldn't help but hate myself for not knowing sooner. I surveyed the last several years of my life and Satan rejoiced in trying to convince me I was always going to be the "Precious Moments, sitting in the parking lot, no religious jewelry" kind of girl.

And I believed him more times than I care to admit.

I would sit in the back of other Bible study groups for years to come, hungry for knowledge but not for the fellowship of others. They were all incredibly nice but I had a feeling they were going to hate me once they found out the truth.

I was a sinner. A wretched, ugly, dirty, sin-filled girl with a past that would make them run.

In my head I knew that it was gone, that I was made pure by Him, but my heart couldn't comprehend it. Truth be told, I still struggle with it sometimes. I don't think I'm alone in that.

It took me awhile to finally sit down with some other believers and share the burden I was carrying. I felt better once I had. It's a difficult thing to try and move ahead and stop beating yourself up for what you used to be.

We all feel like there is something from our past that could pop up and ruin us. We believe that if people really knew who we had been, they wouldn't love us anymore. They would judge us and look at us like the one who "barely made it into the club."

None of that is necessarily true, but it doesn't change the way it feels. You have probably had a moment where you sat in a group of people with whom you don't really feel like you belong. I am convinced that the enemy preys on our memories and regrets, and taunts us with the many ways in which we have failed God.

The gospel of grace is so simple that it's hard to believe.

What kind of economy is this? One Man suffers on my behalf and what I get out of it is a clean slate and a pure heart? I know better than to think I deserve that exchange.

I know exactly what I have done to grieve Him, and I must take Him at His word when He says that my sins are as far away from being held against me as the east is from the west.

I don't believe it will honor God for me to go into great detail about my past, but I want you to know that you aren't alone in your shame. The specifics of our sin are not what is important. We each have had seasons where we were trapped in our sin. It is a conscious choice we make to walk away from those places. More often than not, we walk away and then look back because we wonder if we belong there more than here in the land of freedom.

Do not allow yourself to be consumed by your sin, or convinced that you have done something that could so separate you from the Lord that you cannot be restored by Him through Jesus. It is in these moments that we often resort to feeling as though we might as well go on and sin because we aren't ever going to be good anyway. This "all or nothing" mentality will get you nowhere, and the prison that you build around yourself will eventually destroy the hope for redemption and restoration you could have through Christ.

How are we supposed to do this dance of grace, though? How do we live purposeful, God-oriented lives when we have such flawed, sinful humanity?

For the rest of the chapter, I'm going to ask you to come into my home, pull up a cozy chair, and think of me as your friend. I'm the friend that won't judge you, condemn you, or threaten you. It's a safe place for you to be, and I don't want you to leave until you have started to loosen your grip on yesterday.

Which means you may need to reread this chapter a few times.

I've told you about where I've been, and I wonder if while you were reading you've had thoughts of your own difficult seasons. I know how hard it is, but I want you to press through this exercise as you ask the Lord to be with you and bring you His peace.

Specifically pray that Satan would be bound and would have no control over this time. Make sure you have a Bible (Precious Moments works just fine!) near you. It's one thing for me to tell you as a friend that this is Truth, but it's another to have the Word of God available to you to remind you that your Father is speaking to you as well. Spend as long as you can with the Lord, confessing each of the times you can remember that you fell into sin. It might be something that just happened or a time many years ago.

Maybe it's a relationship you know you handled wrong, or choices you made with regard to your virginity, your sobriety, or your integrity. You can't possibly think of everything (and praise God for that!), but ask the Lord to bring those things to mind that stand in the way of your relationship with Him. The first time I did this I immediately thought of two seasons of life where I got really off course. One was before I was a believer and the other was after. I know there are many, many more but I trust that these were the ones that God wanted me to deal with at that time. I allowed myself to grieve the missed opportunities but I didn't give Satan the right to convince me that the Lord couldn't use these times for His glory.

It's hard to believe, isn't it?

He can be glorified in spite of our mistakes.

He can redeem those bitter roots to grow something spectacular, but first you must recognize what needs to be done for that to happen. Being a Christian doesn't mean we have a free pass because we can "ask forgiveness later," but rather that we live the life that is poured out in each moment for the One Who revels in making all things new.

It used to scare me that I was accountable for my sins, but I have come to trust Him in even these matters, knowing that He makes all things work together for the good of those who love Him (Romans 8:28). It might not feel good at the time, but the fruit is a life more closely aligned with Jesus, and that is where restoration lies.

Sometimes the hard part isn't setting it down and surrendering it, but rather resisting the urge to go back to it over and over again. I assure you that the Lord is not glorified when we replay sin in our minds, and I don't think any good can come of it once we have already repented and sought restoration. Instead of becoming consumed with the desire to change that, or to spend my time beating myself up, I do something I think has a lot more power. I write down the sin pattern I am seeing in my life, I look for a Scripture that has to do with this topic, and I ask the Lord to give me a needle for the thread of sin I am seeing run through my choices.

Romans 12:2 reinforces this, "Do not conform any longer to the pattern of this world, but be transformed by the renewing of your mind. Then you will be able to test and approve what God's will is—his good, pleasing, and perfect will."

When I am face-to-face with the kind of choice that usually makes me stumble, after I have gone through this process of conforming my thoughts to those of Truth, I let this go through my mind and I meditate on what God has for me.

When I have His Word in my quiver, I am ready to defend myself against my own weaknesses, calling on the Lord to battle for me.

Fill yourself with verses that speak to temptations you often face, and then commit them to memory. Post them on your mirror, hang them by the front door so you can see them when you leave for the day. Place them in the car, or the back of your closet door, your cubicle at work, or by your phone—wherever you are most likely to engage in behavior that falls short of God's standard. You don't have to be held captive, a prisoner of sin.

The Lord has delighted in the grace that washes you white as snow.

White.
As.
Snow.

***

Lord, we struggle to understand what we have done to deserve the love that sees past our sin. We stand before You as men and women who are aware of their transgressions, anticipating the stones but receiving grace instead. Let us remember as we walk away from this place where we came face-to-face with You that we are here to tell Your story. Strengthen us that we may leave our past in the past and commit our futures to You. Help us move past our own fears and inadequacies, and bring people into our lives who can help love us into a place of accepted restoration. We treasure You as the woman did so many years ago, when You bent down to the sand, not to condemn but to convict. Help us to know the difference, and to walk in light of the way You love us even when we don't love ourselves. Bind the enemy when we start to obsess about the past, lest we start to believe Calvary wasn't enough to heal us. Lord, we thank You for the magnitude of grace which we cannot comprehend . . .

CHAPTER 7

BENEFACTORS

FEAR OF NOT BEING SIGNIFICANT

He was going to die soon, and He knew it.

He gathered His disciples around Him and urged them to remember Him when He was gone. It must have been a sober time as the disciples considered what life would be like without the Man they had come to love so much. Jesus broke bread with the people He had shared life with for the last three years. Surely the taste of death was bitter in His cup.

At the close of the Lord's last supper with His disciples, an argument broke out among the disciples. It is the only time recorded from their travels with Jesus that we see them arguing with each other, and it takes my breath away to consider the subject of the argument. For a moment, envision yourself reclining at the table with the Lord as He shares some of His last words, anticipating a time very soon when He will be betrayed, forsaken, and killed. I can imagine I would want to know exactly when, exactly who, and exactly how. I would probably ask Him to tell me over and over again, all the while trying to figure out a way to protect Him and to make sure I did everything in my power to show Him how much I loved Him.

I would scarcely be able to eat from that table, knowing that His betrayer was nearby. Wouldn't I have done anything to show my devotion to Him? Surely I would have offered to lay down my life for His if it would be permissible.

Wouldn't I?

I would like to say I would.

I bet they would have said the same, but the sad truth is that all the love they could humanly feel for Christ was not enough for them to escape their own fear and selfishness on their own. In a matter of hours, Jesus would be taken, beaten, and hung with arms outstretched to the point of death to bear the penalty for their sin and for ours.

I would love to believe that I would have comprehended the magnitude of this moment; that I would break bread with only thoughts of Him, myself made small in my own eyes.

Instead, they argued.

They weren't expressing rage over His death, or fighting to know how they could serve Him. What they wanted to know in this critical moment was this:

Who is the greatest among us?

Who is Your favorite, Jesus? Who am I in Your eyes?

The cup is passed and the wine is drunk.

And instead of tasting His goodness, they fight over their own fear of insignificance.

It is clear as I thumb my way through the pages of the book of Luke that this is a pivotal scene for them. I can see Jesus in my mind's eye, on the seat that rightly would be a throne. I can't imagine I would have been concerned with myself.

But like the disciples, my fear gets the best of me sometimes. As troubled as I may be for Him, truth be told I am no different from the disciples. In the recesses of my heart, in more moments than I want to admit, I have asked Jesus the same.

Do I matter, Lord? Am I important to You?

And Jesus whispers to me in those moments just as He did to them so long ago, asking the question that speaks right to the heart of the fear.

Who is greater?

I don't know if you're like me, but every night as I climb into bed I have the same conversation with myself, and it starts with these four words: "Did I do enough?" Before I know it I am tangled up in the memories of the day, from the nods I gave to the kids in place of conversation, to the dishes piled high in the sink, to the phone calls I forgot to make and on and on. I torment myself with regret, apologizing to the Lord (and often others) about my shortcomings. I don't want the day to be weighed down with mistakes. Yet, it's easy to feel like I didn't do anything that really mattered the entire day.

It's a constant balancing act, and the bottom line is that I want to walk away from today and every other day with the sense that I knew and fulfilled my purpose. As a writer, I can't help but see my life in a series of pages, all torn up and stapled together in a heap with the hope that there will be more days that were noteworthy than not. If I step back it's easy to see why the pages don't seem to matter; just scribbles on a page that had the potential to be beautiful.

More often than not I spend my time on what I *wish* I had done with the kids, what I *wanted* to do in my time with the Lord, the impact I *could* have had if I would have just gotten my act together. And the image of tattered pages, fresh with intention and promise, can haunt me long into the night. At some point I release it to God, asking Him to work with what I have given and to make the next day better.

I can't tell you how many nights I have snuck up the dark staircase and cracked the door to my kids' rooms to watch them sleep. Their sweaty little heads and deep breaths remind me of the sacred responsibility I have been given as a parent, and I want to do it well. I believe that I have many callings in life, but my greatest burden is shepherding my children into a place where they love and serve the Lord despite my shortcomings.

It's so easy to believe the voice that tells us we could have been better. You know that voice, right? It's the one that reminds us about that other mom we know, the one in a play group or at church who would *never* raise her voice at her kids, would *never* go to bed with a sink full of bowls left over from another "cereal for dinner" night. Sound familiar? Well, I, for one, can become so affected by these doubts about myself that I can't seem to tap into whatever it is that I'm supposed to be doing. I have moments that would certainly get a gold star; brief snippets in a day where I feel like I hit the nail on the head. I have many, many more moments that I want to cross off, rewrite, or erase. It's like a constant tipping of the scales—sometimes in my favor and other times not.

It has taken me so long to really evaluate what this negative thinking is doing to my self-confidence and the way it affects all the roles I have. Recently I caught myself in the middle of this thought pattern and I reflected on what was underneath it all. The years and layers peeled back and I was left with a version of the words with which I began this chapter: "Am I *enough*?"

We long to be significant in this world. We want to be recognized for our gifts and assured that we have made an impact on life around us. We live lives that cry out to be noticed and we feel desperately inadequate when we aren't. Yet, may I suggest to us that our primary problem isn't really the objective contribution being made to society at large or even just the people around us.

The bigger issue is whom I have placed in the front row of my audience.

Suppose it were opening night of my great play and I was allowed to invite anyone I want to come and see me. Because I have spent so much time preparing and I really feel like I am doing something that will matter, I want to have people there whose judgment of me is important. I want a couple groups of people in the audience. I'd want to make sure the kids who told me I was too stupid to earn the part in the play all the way up to my parents who brought me to all of my rehearsals and let me practice in front of them were present. It wouldn't hurt to have the guy who runs the TV station down the road, because what if this is my big break? And also, I should ask my friends to come because they will cheer for me at all the parts that are supposed to be funny. Who else? I know. The girl who wanted this part but didn't get it. Then she can see why I was chosen over her and she will envy me and that will make me bigger, right?

Do you see where I'm going with this?

Who are you performing for?

I don't think I have ever met a single person who could honestly say that they never cared about anyone else's opinion of them. There may have been situations where they were able to dismiss feedback, but it seems that no one is immune. We may be talking, working, parenting, advising, teaching, or any other number of things, but as we go through the motions we don't know how to silence the fear: *"Am I important?"*

It is not wrong to want our lives to matter, in fact if for God's kingdom and glory that can be a godly goal. However, I believe we have erroneously chosen earthly people and things to be the scale on which we judge our progress. Am I as good of a dancer as she is? Did I have the better paper? Was I more effective, more likeable, more intelligent? Was I enough?

We fall prey to the belief that our goal is to get approval and recognition by our neighbors, our clients, or our spouses. Certainly, it's nice to feel like you matter to those around you, but if you are looking to them as a barometer of how you're doing in life, you will run into a couple major obstacles, each of which can lead to sin and despair.

The first is that they are flawed the same way you are and they can't objectively evaluate who you are. They can have insight into what they see of your behavior, but it is God who knows your heart as well as each of your breaths. When we look to others for the assurance and identity confirmation that we are to find from the God who created us, we fail to honor Him rightly and essentially put our hope and comfort in people who are ultimately just as sinful as we are.

The second obstacle is that you automatically put yourself in a position of comparison, which leads to competition, which leads to an altered view of yourself in light of "the winner." Either you will be puffed up in your victory or deflated in your failure, and neither will shape your view of yourself in a way that will lead to glorifying God. God is most glorified when we submit ourselves to Him to be conformed to the image of Christ. It is to Jesus—the perfect manifestation of a significant life—that we can rightly compare ourselves. Whoa! Does that mean we should just beat ourselves up constantly since we'll never meet up to the standard of His perfection? No, it's just the opposite. By comparing ourselves to Him we set out on the wisest path, but we also rest in knowing that when we trust in Him for our salvation, we are sealed with the promise that God *will* complete the work of making us more and more like Him.

The desire to be significant is God-given and, I believe, intended to make us long for the ways in which He chooses to use us. Yet, as I've had conversations with various women about this struggle as well as considered what holds me back, I've concluded that the basic barrier to relying on God for our sense of significance is that in a practical, everyday, standing-on-stage kind of way, He can seem like the One in the back of the auditorium taking notes on your performance but never clapping.

Is that an accurate image of God? No, of course not.

I remember the first time I heard the Bible verse that said God knew how many hairs I had on my head. I didn't think it was impossible for Him, just unlikely to be something that mattered. It was much more plausible that He would know the number of grains of sand on the beaches than the number of hairs I had. And He saves my tears? Why? Why would my tears matter to Him? He has a lot more important things to do than worry about me crying. I struggled (struggle?) with the notion that I really had significance to God.

I wrote that last sentence and I stared at my computer, tempted to erase it and say something more spiritual because I know very well that the Bible tells me I matter. I have learned at least 11 songs that tell me so.

But do I believe it?

Better yet, do I *live* it?

Or is it more likely that I wouldn't have even asked Jesus to come to my stupid opening night because I have a feeling He is going to be at the symphony house downtown or busy with His plans for someone way more important than me.

And quite frankly, I would rather not give Him the chance to forget me.

In some sense I think we rely on other people to tell us if we matter or not because, well, at least we know they'll show up.

I want to be worth noticing, to be a priority, to feel like I am appreciated and respected. I want to believe I did something great with my life, and what if He doesn't even care?

I will tell you a true story as long as you promise not to hold it against me. Because, you know, your opinion of me is paramount.

When I was in junior high school, a friend of mine asked me to go to church with her family the following Sunday. I agreed because she told me they had fruit punch and homemade cookies.

For the record, they had neither.

I sat through what was quite possibly the longest sermon known to man (or at least a junior high girl), and I focused my attention on the 150-year-old woman in the front row the entire time because I was convinced that she had died in the middle of his talk. At one point she kind of snorted and sat upright while smacking her tongue around her mouth and I felt relief wash over me.

I mean, who would want to die on a turquoise seat cushion? Not I, friend. *Not I.*

Needless to say I didn't hear much of what the pastor was saying, but on the way home I listened to them discussing it and was fascinated by the conversation. At one point I asked my friend's mother to explain what she was saying, and she replied, "Because we matter to God, Angie. That's what John 3:16 is all about."

I still remember the smell of leather in the Volvo wagon as I nodded to her from the backseat, watching her eyes in the rearview mirror as she tried to decide if I was bluffing.

I most certainly was.

I had no idea what she was talking about, but I did a little research later in the week. And, being the classic overachiever I am, I committed the whole verse to memory before the next

Sunday so I could impress her with my stellar Bible knowledge. I'm a theater nerd, remember? Memorizing is my middle name.

I'm pretty sure they were all dazzled with my recitation of that nugget of truth, and I considered it a raging success.

Until we pulled up into my driveway and she put the car in park and turned to face me.

"Do you know what that *means*, hon?"

"Mmm-hmm. Yeah. I definitely do." I reached for the handle of the car, my face growing redder as I realized I was not prepared for the inevitable follow-up question.

"Good. I think it's very important for you to know that Jesus died for you." She smiled and nodded her head as if to dismiss me.

I started to step out but the thought was so perplexing to me that I closed the door and asked her to clarify that last part. She did, and as I sat in the back of the hot car I distinctly remember having one of my first deep theological thoughts.

That is the most ridiculous thing I have ever heard in my life, lady.

I didn't say it out loud, in fact I continued to "mmm-hmm" with gusto, nodding like my head was going to snap off my neck. Clearly this woman was crazier than I had given her credit for and the goal for me should be to just get to my front porch safely.

I don't think I said anything else of substance to her, but later that night I sat at the dinner table after everything had been cleared away and I told my parents about my little car talk.

I also stood and recited my new Bible verse like I was in the running for an Academy Award. As I recall, there was wild applause and great pride at my prowess.

It made for a dramatic monologue, that's for certain, but whether or not it was *true* was a different story. And whether or not it was true *for me* was absolutely out of the question.

"Isn't that nuts?" I asked my dad because he was the smartest person I knew and surely he would back me up and tell me I never had to ride in the Volvo of eternal salvation again.

"What part of it is nuts to you, Angela?"

Umm, I have an idea. How about the "all of it" part? I thought.

As you have probably already surmised, I love a good question.

And as I considered how to respond to my dad's question, I was surprised. I didn't know if there had been a man who was really the Son of God. Maybe. Could He have been born in a manger to a virgin? I guess. What about all the miracles and all that? Sure, that's possible. Seth Manillo shoved an entire chicken potpie in his mouth at lunch a couple days ago and that was pretty unlikely. I had aced a math test, which was tantamount to winning the lottery without buying a ticket. So, as I considered this possibility it didn't seem completely ridiculous.

Well, it did seem ridiculous, but not impossible.

I mean, if He was real I don't see why that stuff couldn't have happened. And the idea that someone would die for another person? Sure. If my dad saw a bullet coming toward my mom, he would jump in front of it without a second thought. So it wasn't out of the question.

I still hadn't answered my dad, so I started to mumble what I was thinking and it dawned on me that I could actually believe this ridiculous story. In fact, I might even reconsider my boycott of the little church if they would invest in a gallon or two of fruit punch.

That wasn't the problem with the whole God story thing.

It wasn't about Him at all, in fact.

I believed He could do it, I just didn't believe He would do it *for me.*

At the heart of the issue is the feeling that we could never be significant enough to benefit from the thorns that cut into His skin and the suffering He experienced as the sky grew dark on a hill in Calvary.

Why?

Because I have never done anything to deserve a love like that.

And do you know what He says in response?

You have never been so right in your life, child.

My view of significance relies on performance reports and my children's behavior. It is dependant on where I fall on the totem pole of achievement and financial success. It is bound to convince me I'm not worth it.

And do you know what He says to that?

Now that is where I draw the line.

Sitting at a table across from my father as a twelve-year-old, I realized that I wasn't sure I could believe in a God who would choose *me.*

Through the years I have butted up against this doubt, and I would love to say I have moved past it. At certain times it's easier than others but I must confess that even then it is based on my interpretation of what makes me worthy, and that is not God's economy for value.

It's why we love the clean slate, the New Year's resolutions, the beginning of a semester, and the way the moonlight falls on our children's faces while they rest.

Because we feel like we still have another chance to make a mark.

Erik Erikson, a well-known psychologist, studied the phases of life and created what he felt like were different stages we go through as we age. He believed that as we near the end of our lives we begin to reflect on what we have done with our days and we will either have integrity or despair. His definition of integrity was based on the idea that we could look back with contentment and feel fulfilled through a deep sense that life has meaning and we have made a contribution. On the other hand, despair is the sense that our retrospection leads us to focus on failures and regret, and that we can easily grow depressed at our lack of "success."

We struggle with significance because we want to know that we are living out our purpose, being obedient to what we have been called to do. We want to believe that we will leave this earth better for having been here. We can become stuck thinking that we could have done more, or that we never did the thing we were supposed to do. Looking at the pages of our lives, we can conclude that the book we have labored over was an epic flop. Forget the *New York Times* best-seller list—we just want to know someone, *anyone,* even took the time to read it.

And yet, I see the Man who took on my sin, twisted in form and sweating with grief as He suffered for me.

For *me.*

To the degree that I can comprehend this is the degree to which I will live my life as a woman who desires to bring His name great glory. That single, solitary thought is enough for me to focus my eyes on something I may have never noticed before.

My sweet Jesus; the One Who watches me from the back of the theater while He marvels at the girl who told Him she would never believe in the script.

And while she performs for all the people, He sees her need to be recognized and affirmed. And as the curtain comes down a bit later, He won't be consumed by the lines she missed or the way she had failed Him or stumbled through the scene.

He will be reading the next line, the taste of love on His breath as He stands and whispers for only her to hear, *"Well done, my good and faithful servant . . . well done . . ."*

―――――

How many of our days have we spent at the table with Christ, tucked away in the upper room as we wonder who we are in His eyes? And how many days have we also spent comparing ourselves to those around us, desperate to be considered better because we have convinced ourselves that this is the measure of our worth? It does me good to know that even in His physical presence, His disciples had some of the same thoughts I do. It wasn't that they didn't love Him—by all accounts they loved Him as much as they were capable. But in our hedonistic, "me, me, me" world, we can't help but take the opportunity to confirm our place whenever we can. And who better to declare us worthy than Jesus Himself?

So we sit at the table and we look at those around us with eyes of competition and jealousy. We wrongly believe that we are in a race with them for the affections of our Savior and the praise of our fellow man.

Jesus cuts to the quick with His response, and as I have prayed over these words I can feel my spirit leap at the freedom He has promised to those who will take hold of their true calling.

"The kings of the Gentiles exercise lordship over them, and those in authority over them are called benefactors. But not so with you. Rather, let the greatest among you should be like the youngest, and the one who rules like the one who serves. For who is greater, the one who is at the table or the one who serves? Is it not the one who is at the table? But I am among you as one who serves" (Luke 22:25–27 ESV).

The "benefactors" are the ones who have a measure of power, and they are in charge of distributing land and such to the soldiers. They were considered the authority over the one to whom they were bequeathing these items. Jesus is clear in saying that we are not to be benefactors, lording over others, but rather servants who consider themselves nothing.

Who are you trying to be?

God Himself chose to be the servant, and He wants us to consider this as we run the race of life. It's so easy to feel like a place at the head of the table makes us important and gives us a feeling of accomplishment, and it *is* entirely possible—likely, even—that our neighbors and coworkers will judge us based on seating arrangement. We may become so consumed with the limelight that we miss the gaze of our Savior, intently focused on the one with her hands in the soapy water.

She is not esteemed by those around her, in fact, they may consider her their subordinate in many ways. Instead of fighting this belief and asserting herself as worthy, she bows lower and lower until she can scarcely be seen. And there, at the foot of the Good Shepherd, she rejoices in knowing that she has loved in a manner worthy of the King. We have grown weary trying to impress people, and we walk away with a sense of emptiness that belies our intent.

I have met the maidservant of Christ in many faces and I have reveled at the peace that accompanies those who care not to be seated. As the days pass and the dishes pile high, might I be the one who ties my apron tight and disregards public opinion? I pray so, and I pray the same for you.

We are significant in our insignificance, urged to have the faith of a child and the heart of a servant. And be assured, friend, that you are loved in a way that is infinitely different than any love you could know here on earth. It is the love of a Man who had the chance to exert His importance in the eyes of the world, and instead did exactly what He calls us to do.

Serve, sacrifice, love.

And be made great for His glory.

———————————

Father God, I want to start with an apology to You for all the times I have misstepped in this area. I don't want to be so caught up in my own definition of significance that I miss the opportunity to serve You. Help me turn my head from those who rely on the world to define them, and restore me to a place where I rejoice in knowing You think I was worth creating. All of us long to be used by You and to reject the world's notion of success, but it is a challenge. Remind us daily that You know what it is like to be a servant, and to submit to the will of the Father. Bow our knees when we refuse, Lord. Thank You for loving us into this life, and for the grace that covers our sin.

CHAPTER 8

APPOINTED

FEAR OF GOD'S PLAN FOR MY LIFE

─────────────────────────

"Arise," came the voice of the Lord. "Go to Ninevah . . ." (Jonah 1:2 ESV).

Ninevah.

Sprawled out on the Eastern bank of the Tigris River, it was a hub of wealth and disobedience. The opulent Assyrian culture had little time to worry about the warnings of destruction, as they were too busy living the good life. I imagine them dripping in jewels, soaked with hedonism as they laughed in the face of God.

It seems Jonah felt the same.

So when the Lord told him to go and confront them about their evil ways, he resisted. It is possible he was frightened, but even more likely that he didn't want to see them repent. As far as Jonah was concerned, they could all just die in their own filth while people who really lived with their hearts bowed to God would prosper.

Obviously, Jonah didn't agree with God's reasoning about Ninevah, because despite the explicit instructions he had received, an *itty-bitty-teeny-weeny-maybe-He-won't-even-notice-this* word shapes the rest of his life:

But.

Was he confused about where he was supposed to go? Nope.

Did he know why he was supposed to go there? Yep.

Is it possible he was more confident in his own plan than he was in God's?

I think we all know the answer to that question, and we also know what happens when we ignore the calling of God in order to pursue what we see as a better plan.

If we're lucky, we get swallowed.

═══════

I never wanted to be in the cemetery at all, let alone watch them lower her into the ground.

My daughter.

She had lived for two hours outside of my body, which was more than we thought we would get with her. And yet, despite all the pleading with God to heal her, we found ourselves draped in black under a cloudless sky, listening to our pastor talk about death. Her death.

Belly still swollen, I laid my head on Todd's shoulder and felt the sun beat down on my face. I had prayed for beautiful weather and in a sense I was relieved. I was also furious that the sun felt the liberty to try and cast light here where the shadows danced.

What a hideous mess.

I would have said I trusted God, but staring into the

three-foot-long space freshly opened in the earth for my sweet baby, I wondered if I had been a fool.

I felt dizzy in the heat, desperate to make sense out of the fact that I wouldn't see her again. I would never hear her voice or even know what color her eyes were. I was surrendering her to the God who ordained her to be mine. And she wasn't mine at all.

There were moments when He could have changed it all. I remember staring at the lights in the operating room as they looked her over. I waited, believing she could still be okay despite all the months and the tests.

I didn't give up that hope, but here in the bright sun, where the grass withered and the tears fell, I had to face reality.

My plan was not God's plan.

And quite frankly, I liked mine a whole lot better.

It wasn't the last time I would see a baby buried there. The following month after my nephew died in his sleep, we gathered again, begging for mercy as the promises of God felt more like wishful thinking than guarantees.

We released balloons and watched them fly until they got so small we could only imagine what they would have been. I didn't want to let mine go, because it was hard to watch them disappear. Of course, I eventually did. We all do.

I would be lying if I said I never questioned Him, and I don't believe He begrudged me because of it. How could I, a mother and an aunt, walk away from those two days believing He had everything under control and I need not fear?

We say it in so many beautiful ways, and we nod our heads in sympathy, reciting the age-old sentence that should bring us more peace than confusion.

"His ways are not our ways . . ."

It looks great in a card store, but it feels hollow in a graveyard.

Bitter sun, glaring at me as I wonder how I will return to this place where death won. I despise it even today as I consider what could have been. Who can blame us for getting tangled up in our fleshly love as we mourn the losses that come with this life? We were made to love, and as our arms wrap around the air in a desperate embrace, we see that it is all a vapor after all.

We are left, some of us, with our new black dresses and another stack of questions to pass along to God.

Maybe it wasn't a black dress for you.

Maybe you always longed for a white one, but despite your years of earnest prayer and trust in God, you find yourself alone. You cook dinner for yourself as the TV blares the news in the background and you wonder why He didn't give you the life you dreamed. You go to church, but as the man in front of you slips his arm around his wife you can't help but wonder if the blessings stopped after pew #5.

Or maybe you are that wife, and as his arm rests on you, you fight the urge to storm out of the back door, screaming for all the church to see that he has betrayed you. You found the letters written to a woman whose face you don't need to see to know is more beautiful than you will ever be. You let him hold you because there are people watching and you need them to believe a little while longer. Underneath it all you know you are a fool for believing it would ever work out.

And what of that woman? The one who imagined she would be married herself one day? She was somebody's mistress, and she woke up with her face in the hot shower, wondering how she had managed to get herself into this situation. She loved the Lord, always had. She had grown up the daughter of a man who told her she could do no right, and the backside of his belt never disagreed. She remembers the sting of the leather, pale in comparison to the words he told her. Pale, even, to the way she believed them.

She was the last in a string of unwanted daughters, and as she feels her skin scorching under the water she doubts there is a God who would rescue her from this life.

I know a woman who has prayed for more than two decades that she will hold her own child. As the years pass and the pregnancy tests stack up in the trash, she can't help but despise her own reflection. She feels like a failure, and she wants to know why it is that a woman three miles down the road had a baby, only to purposely leave her in the car to die.

The relentless sun shines light in the crevices we have in our own lives, and on the abundance that everyone else seems to have. We alternate between feelings of helplessness and fury as we stare into the ground, his eyes, her youth, the empty cradle, the empty bed, and the face in the mirror, hollow with fear.

His ways are not our ways.

I believe that.

But I certainly don't always like it.

Maybe you can relate. Maybe you don't even go to church because you have given up on Him. You watch the local news and you can't help but question the One behind the chaos. You have seen enough of the dark to ignore the light, and you would rather rely on yourself than the God who is watching it all unfold.

Or maybe, you're like me.

I believe fully, wholeheartedly, maddeningly, in the goodness of God.

I just don't always feel like it applies to me.

I stand a few feet from a miracle baby, a rescued marriage, a victory against sickness, and I bask in the glow of Him. On the other hand, I cower in the face of His plans for me, often deliberately slipping out from underneath Him so I can be in control.

It's an ugly thing to feel like the rest of the world has His favor and you have only the dewy grass beneath you and the anger beside you.

I deserve better than this.

I don't deserve any of this.

I deserve a chance.

I deserve what she has.

I don't deserve a single thing.

I am entitled to a life that consists of more than hospital meals and midnight prayer.

Why doesn't He take notice of me and help? He is so capable with others and yet His arms reach just short of me.

Have you felt that way? Have you ever been afraid to truly trust His plan for you without something else on which to fall back?

I have.

I do.

I want it, that love that says *I don't care what happens as long as You're with me.*

I want to walk with Him and nothing else, confident that He only has my best at heart. But it seems so quiet here in the silence, and I'm tempted more often than I care to admit to believe that my life is a jumbled mass of plan B's.

And underneath that is the nagging voice that has lured me toward despair: *I would have done it better than this, Lord.*

I won't pretend to know why God allows the suffering He does. I can read dozens of verses that tell me, but deep inside me it still aches. I struggle to make sense of how a loving God could let a three-year-old child place a wreath of flowers on her mother's casket.

I also struggle with understanding how God could watch them put a crown of thorns on His own Son.

"There is goodness that will come from all of this." I whisper to the empty room, barely believing it myself. I wonder if you have stood there too.

I am tempted to give you Scripture, give you advice, give you the solution that will clothe you in peace, but I don't listen to it myself sometimes.

Do we have a right to be angry about tragedies and that which clearly seems to be an injustice? Should we shake our fists at

God and tell Him He has made a mess of it all? Maybe we should just abandon Him altogether. Or chalk it up to our past, our doubt, our fear, our unworthiness, our failures. Chalk it up to a God who had better things to do with His time than worry about finding you a husband or allowing my daughter to be healed.

His ways are not our ways . . .

And yet every day, in ways big and small, we tell Him we have a better way.

We manipulate whatever we can get our hands on as we fall to the temptation to believe He has forgotten us. Instead of loving our neighbors, we decide to love what they have and what they don't have to face. We confirm in our own minds that we are the exception to the rule of love and grace. We crucify Him over and over again with our resentment.

The Bible is littered with stories of people who believed they had a better solution than the one God was offering to them. What we notice upon reading these stories is that the Lord doesn't respond the same way to each one; it seems that individuals who plead their case to Him while expressing a genuine desire to remain in His will have influenced His response.

For example, when Abraham pleaded to God on behalf of a sinful, disobedient city, we see them "negotiating" about the number of righteous men that must be found in order to save that city. Throughout the conversation we see Abraham humbling himself to the Lord, saying things like, "though I am nothing but dust and ashes . . ." (Genesis 18:27) and "may the Lord not be angry" (Genesis 18:32). Abraham wanted God to change what He had already told him, but it is also abundantly clear that Abraham knew who is God and who was not. Abraham recognized in this moment what I fail to so many times in my life.

I have every right in the world to ask God to intervene if it is still in accordance with the purpose of His will.

But I must kneel low before Him in humble submission, recognizing that at the end of the day, it just might not look the way I want it to. The beautiful, difficult love between our Savior and us is magnified for the world when we remain in this posture of deference. What a beautiful image we allow Him to paint when we trust Him in seasons of life that feel ugly.

After all, our Lord did the same.

As His blood mingled with sweat and the hours passed in the garden, He knew He would soon be crucified. Three times He asked His Father to let the cup pass if He was willing. Even in the face of death, Jesus recognized the sovereignty of God and submitted to it saying, "yet not my will, but yours be done" (Luke 22:42).

For most of us, the setting isn't quite this dramatic. Yet, we are called to say the same—no matter how small the circumstance. Perhaps you aren't facing a crisis in this season, but you certainly have the opportunity to build up your faith while you go about your day. It sounds strange, but there is great comfort and strength in intentionally seeking the Lord's will as you live life. You don't just have to be at the end of your rope to cry out to Him. In fact you may not recognize His leading in that moment if you haven't relied on Him before.

What if we deliberately made the Lord a part of our hours and not just our hour of need?

A woman once asked me if I thought it was silly that she asked for a toy to be on sale for her son. She explained that she felt ridiculous praying for something that trivial when there were so many other important things going on in the world. We had a giggle together as we imagined God multitasking as only we can imagine it, and we discussed the way He desires to be a part of the mundane.

As Christians we can look ridiculous to the outside world when we say we "prayed for a parking spot," or "asked the Lord to get us there in time." It does sound silly when compared to the heavy issues being faced if not by us, then by those around us.

I am certainly not making the case for a "gumball machine God" who gives us whatever we ask. Rather, I want to encourage you to invite Him into your days. Speak to Him while you do the laundry, play with your children, or sit in a stadium full of people.

Be in constant communion with Him so that when times get hard, you will have relationship instead of requests.

So many people (including myself) have felt seasons of separation from the Lord, and struggle to hear Him in the midst of the mess of life. I want to have the kind of life with God that allows me to rest in Him. Period. Rest in Him. Daily. Hourly. Moment-by-moment, not crisis-to-crisis. That life comes from intentional, earnest, devoted choices to love Him and seeking to know Him better. As we do so, our lives begin to have a different rhythm. Then, when things turn upside-down we feel more like we are confiding in a close friend than a faraway, much-too-busy-to notice-or-care, God.

As we lean into Him, the most precious, inexplicable change begins to shape our decisions. We find that we desire to exist in accordance with His will and our prayers take on a new intensity. We tap into the source of all things good when we align our goals with His plans.

As unbelievable as it feels sometimes, God hasn't taken the day off and left you to fend for yourself in the midst of a world spinning wildly out of control. I don't know why my daughter died, and I doubt I will ever fully know while I live on this earth. I have seen glimpses of the goodness that has come from the fruit of her life, but I am still left with the ache of loss. I try to seek the will of God and make myself small in the wake of confusion. He has met me in my grief and I have treasured His presence even when I didn't understand why He allowed it. We will likely be tempted to believe that God fails us as life crumbles around us. We might choose to give into that temptation, concluding that He is cold and uncaring of our plight. In reality, if we are walking through life in relationship with Him, we know better. It isn't a naïve trust that belies common sense, but rather the abiding love that comes only from knowing the God of the universe intimately.

Throughout the day, regardless of the context, I find myself whispering, "Help me, Lord," or "Guide me, Lord." I ask Him to speak, and His presence leads me to seek Him more and more. It isn't complicated, but we miss so many opportunities to gain wisdom when we rely on our limited cognizance.

I desire to be perfectly in step and at peace with the will of God. I ask Him to grant me that every chance I can. You can, too.

Even if our intentions are good, we will sometimes fail to understand and obey the will of God. Sometimes it can really "feel" like the right thing. Or, perhaps we do hear Him, but we justify our actions by pretending we know something He might not. In our blissful rebellion we march west when He says east.

And He does what any good Father would do.

With the most tender love we could ever know, He reminds us of the dark place, many years ago, where a man sat in the belly of a fish and believed God's love was seen in His purpose for him.

———

The word *appointed* is used four times in the ESV translation of the book of Jonah. We first see it as the Lord appoints, or "provides" as the NIV states, a large fish (potentially a whale) to swallow Jonah.

I never had a flannel board as a child, but if I had, I imagine the fish would be seen as the antagonist in the story. I picture him angry and out for blood as he gobbles up poor Jonah. It took me many years (and still no flannel board) to see what God was really saying in this story.

He *provided* the fish.

Not to harm Jonah, but to *rescue* him.

He knew Jonah's heart, so He did something drastic, something epic, something that to the naked eye looks like a tragedy, and He used it for His glory.

The words of Jonah are profound in their earnest simplicity:

> "So I said, 'I have been expelled from Your sight. *Nevertheless* I will look again toward Your holy temple.'" (Jonah 2:4 NASB, emphasis mine)

I want to live the "nevertheless" life, don't you?

Many times in my life I have seen an obstacle as the enemy, but looking back now I see it was an appointed mercy.

We can't whitewash all the hurt in life, throw it in a pile, and say, "Well there. It's all fixed now and I'll never be sad or confused about God's will for me again." It is a constant dying to self that leads us into the place of trust, and sometimes it looks a whole lot like the guts of a fish.

Nevertheless . . .

Jonah was human and suffered the same temptation to fall back into patterns of disobedience as do we. Despite his eloquent speech and ultimate obedience to go to Ninevah, the second time he was asked, he still had a little trouble. Jonah continued to express his frustration over the fact that the Ninevites have repented, essentially telling God that he was mad that God has had mercy on those wicked people.

Wait.

What?

Weren't you just inside a gigantic fish telling Him how great His mercies were? And now you're furious and informing God that this was what you were afraid of as though you are now justified in your original act of disobedience?

He concludes his rant with the old "I would rather be dead"

trick for dramatic effect, and waits for God to respond to his junior-high-esque tantrum.

I would be tempted to laugh at him if I weren't standing in his shoes.

God's response is a question I have to face every single day I live in a place of anger, thinking I know better than He does.

"Do you have good reason to be angry?" (Jonah 4:4 NASB).

Yikes.

Well, I was pretty sure I did.

Jonah left town (I picture it in a huff, but that might be because I have flannel-board envy) and ended up east of the city in a shelter he made for himself so he could stay out of the hot sun. Jonah had taken matters into his own hands, and fresh from his exit cue, he set up shop in a spot that afforded him a view of Tarshish so he can see what happens to the Ninevites.

I believe I have made the same shelter on more than one occasion in my life.

See me, God? I'm fine. I made this little life and I can watch You work from here, where I'm in control. You go ahead and forgive everyone since clearly You have no desire for justice. I mean, they disobeyed You. They should pay the price! I can't sit idly by and watch all of these hooligans receive mercy. It's too much.

And this grace-spilling God just can't help but teach Jonah one more lesson before it's over.

The sun is scorching him like it does in a graveyard on a clear spring day.

And God appoints a plant to protect Jonah. As he embraces the cool shade, grateful for the provision, we see the dance continue. Jonah is happy in the shade until the following day, when God appoints a worm to attack and destroy the plant, thereby leaving Jonah miserable again in the heat. Then God appoints a scorching wind, which leads Jonah to lament again that death would be better than this life.

Is it a game to God? Does He just want to see what we will do in response? No, of course not. He wants us to answer the question.

"Do you have good reason to be angry about the plant?" (Jonah 4:9 NASB).

He's not messing around with this anger thing, is He? And why?

Because He wants to remind us of our place. He knows our misguided, flawed, whale-sized feelings of entitlement to run the show need to be exposed.

God loves my daughter Audrey more than I do.

He appointed her to me.

He appointed the whale, the plant, the worm, the wind, the breath in her body.

Not to harm me, but because of His wild grace.

I don't want it to sound trite, but I need you to hear me say this as a woman who has screamed out from the pain of death. I want her to be alive and resting in her room as I write these words. I want the story to be different, and lest I am tempted to believe I deserve an explanation, I remind myself that He who allowed the vine to wither was the same One Who grew it into being and brought it life in the first place.

And when the sun burns my eyes and the wind whips me into a place of doubt, I have committed to return to a place of worship.

A place where it is too dark to see anything but Him. A place too quiet to hear anything other than the sound of my own praise.

"Nevertheless I will look again toward Your holy temple, Lord . . ."

And like the bird that can only learn to sing in the dark, I will follow the sound of my Master, urging me to walk in faith and trust, regardless of what the world is doing around me.

And there, in the land of promise, I will rest my weary bones and cease to fear His hand on me.

I will believe in spite of the vine that I cannot control.

Because I trust the Maker who told me I was worth more than a sparrow. Because He loved me enough to rescue me when I thought I would never see the light of day again.

Because His ways, you know . . .

They aren't ours.

━━━━━━━━

Father, help us to believe You are the Author and Perfecter of our lives. We don't want to react out of doubt, and we don't want to live under our self-made structures. We want to hear Your voice, to be obedient in response, and to be grateful for that which You have appointed us. Be with each of us when we find ourselves trapped in the belly of a fish, flailing for freedom and tempted to despair. This which we see as impossible is nothing more than an opportunity to return to You and bring You glory. Thank You for Your mercy and Your patience as we fail over and over again, believing we have a better way. Who are we to deserve a God who is so gracious with His love? May we seek Your will over ours every day, and may we never forget the God who provides both the sun and the shade.

CHAPTER 9

BEGINNING TO SINK

FEAR THAT GOD ISN'T REAL

They were still reeling with excitement over the Master's work. It had looked like an impossible situation just a few hours before and then they found themselves gathered together, in awe of what He had done. I imagine they retold the story from each of their perspectives as they remembered the way He had provided food for all the people.

"It was only five loaves! I saw it myself."

"And two fish. That's it. And look what He did! I knew He was the One."

Five thousand people ate from these meager offerings, and the disciples had watched it unfold, no doubt basking in the glow of Jesus' divinity. They didn't have long to reminisce as Jesus told them to go on ahead so He could spend time in prayer with His

Father. They complied and got into a boat as He finished dismissing the people.

At about three o'clock in the morning, the disciples had gotten rather far from where they expected Jesus to be. At that moment, they saw a man walking on the water, coming closer and closer to them. The disciples became terrified, believing it to be a ghost. Jesus responded immediately, saying, "Take courage! It is I. Don't be afraid" (Matthew 14:27).

I don't think it is any coincidence that this story unfolds in the wake of seeing Jesus perform a miracle. What a beautiful reminder that even for those who walked alongside the Lord, it can be easy to forget His power when fear creeps into our minds.

I imagine the boat being tossed about in the waves as the moon barely illuminated the Man walking toward them, and suddenly the voice of Peter cried out, "If it's you, tell me to come to you on the water" (Matthew 14:28).

If?

He just told them who He was, and it seems like they would know His voice after all this time with Him. But this time it was different. It wasn't a sick girl or people waiting to be fed; it was them.

And maybe, like Peter, we find it much easier to believe His deity when we're on land, safe and sound as He provides for others. When push comes to shove and we find ourselves miles away from shore, we want to believe it is Him coming to us, but we often question it. Jesus? Is that You?

A deeper, more profound question begs an answer; the question that leads to all others in our mind:

"Are You even real?"

It seems Peter had the kind of heart that strayed from his Master despite his love for Jesus. He is the same disciple who will deny Christ three times later in the Gospels, and the one who impetuously tries to defend the Lord by cutting off the ear of a soldier who is threatening Christ. I smile when I read of Peter because I see so much of myself in him. I throw myself into the arms of God, wooed by the love song He has sung over me and eager to share it with the rest of the world. I am zealous to be His servant and devoted to Him as passionately as one could be.

And yet, there have been more times than I care to admit when I lie restless in my bed long after the house is quiet and I ask myself if this whole thing is a sham.

For someone who likes to squeeze the facts out like a wet towel while confirming my data with at least ten backup sources, it can be a scary place to be. And like Peter, I cry out to the One I believe is Him, saying, "If it is You . . ."

I choke on my words, afraid to admit I have wondered, ashamed that my litmus test relies so much on my perception. As the Lord did with Peter, He answers me time and time again with one simple word.

"Come."

With faith I step out, eyes on Him and mind steadied by His voice. My feet are moving and for a moment I wonder why I ever doubted. What mortal could call me to walk on water? I am safe with Him; I am His . . .

Peter grew confident as he approached the Lord, and I imagine he began to forget his fears as he did the impossible. It isn't long, though, before he takes his eyes off the Lord and realizes that the wind is creating chaos.

He is drowning fast, and he has only a split-second to make a choice that will change the rest of his life.

I was in the second grade and we had been ushered into the school library for a special presentation. I spent several years of my childhood in Kobe, Japan, and this was my first Christmas overseas.

I went to an International school so I had friends from all over the world, which afforded me some really cool opportunities to learn about different cultures. I preferred the library to every other part of the school, including the recess area. We all whispered and tried to stay calm as we slipped into the great big room and saw paper snowflakes dancing from the ceiling. A Swedish sixth grader was standing on a small platform and she had several wooden toys gathered around her. Her name was Anya and she was beautiful. She was tall and had long blonde hair, which was presently adorned with a crown of lit candles.

The lights were dimmed in the library and she stood very, very still as we found places to sit near her. She smiled like an angel and I remember being mesmerized by her flowing white robe and the way the candles gently flickered. I waved to her. She didn't wave back, which was fine because I was a little concerned about the fire risk given the fact that there was a lot of paper around. I nodded and stuck my thumb up as if to say, "It's fine. Stay safe, girl."

I thought about what it would be like to be in Anya's family. She had five sisters and they all looked like the exact same girl in six different stages. Her father was a physician and her mother made sugar cookies with the fat sugar crystals on top. Her sister was in my class and she saw me waving. She glared at me and leaned in my direction.

"Anya isn't Anya right now. She is *Lucia*. Don't distract her."

"Okay, sorry. Who's Lucia?" She put her finger to her lips and hushed me, turning back to her sister with a knowing grin.

I told her not to hush me but I said it louder than I meant to, and Anya "Lucia" closed her eyes like she was trying to regroup.

I crossed my legs and waited for the presentation to begin; annoyed that Mrs. Barton was staring at me like I was the problem when clearly the girl with a flaming crown was the one to watch.

A few moments later the lights dimmed even further and we all gasped as Anya sat herself down on a stool very slowly.

I glanced back at Mrs. Barton to see if we should be concerned for our safety. It was too dark to see her very well and I started getting a little nervous, so I thought about Charlie Brown. I don't know exactly why but he was my "go-to" thought when I got scared. Well, him or books, but it was way too dark to see those.

"*My name is Lucia . . .*" she began.

Twenty-three second graders held their breath as a collective whole. I grabbed my friend Natalie's leg. She put her hand on mine and I could feel her sweating.

I was pretty sure I was never going to escape. Honestly, I was terrified. *Charlie Brown, Snoopy, nothing to fear . . .*

"Many years ago, I died for my faith in Jesus Christ." She held one tall candle in her hands, and as she spoke she lifted it closer to her face to enhance the creepiness factor.

Forget Charlie Brown. I'm going to die in the library.

I reached up and started to twist my hair around my fingers, barely stopping myself from putting the other thumb in my mouth because everyone would see me.

"Many people don't know who I am, but I want to tell you the story of my life and then I will allow you to ask me questions." Anya smiled a little but I was still relatively certain she was the angel of death.

She told us all about how she was from Sicily. She said that her mother had been sick so she went to some other place to pray for her. While there God told her to be a Christian. Some other people didn't want her to be a Christian so they decided to try and set her on fire. At this point she closed her eyes and pretended to be talking while the flames overtook her.

"I refuse to say I don't believe! I love Jesus! *I love Jesus!*"

Mrs. Barton was mouthing the words with her. *These two were a bunch of fruitcakes,* I thought. But it was still scary because it was real fire and all.

Suddenly Anya snapped her eyes open and they grew wide with mock agony.

"And then, someone put a sword through her neck but she still didn't stop saying she loved Jesus." She went back into closed-eye, freaky Lucia mode and did something that sounded like a chant. Mrs. Barton shook her head from side to side in awe.

As for me, I was just confused and thinking we should flip on the lights and grab a book about Ramona or Laura Ingalls. I started shifting around uncomfortably, trying to decide if I should ask for a bathroom pass before her head started spinning on its axis.

Suddenly I realized Anya's sister was gone and there was singing coming from behind Juvenile Fiction.

All five of her sisters emerged and walked, one after another, in a somber procession toward the platform. They each held a candle and looked straight ahead, completely absorbed in their roles.

When they got to the platform they all rotated toward us and I decided that they were the scariest clone sisters I had ever known. Even the promise of fat sugar crystals wasn't going to be enough to get me to their house ever again.

Anya continued talking for several more minutes about other traditions and eventually she asked the librarian to turn on the lights. Mrs. Barton blew out her head-candles and praised her for the excellent reenactment. All the other girls blew out the candles they were holding and scurried back behind the bookshelf again.

"And now, class, you may ask Anya any questions you would like about how her family celebrates Christmas." Mrs. Barton was flushed with pride, eager to see what other divine wisdom Anya would share with us.

Cyril raised his hand.

"Can I have a candle?"

Mrs. Barton shook her head disapprovingly and motioned for him to put his hand down so someone with a smarter question could have a chance.

Nora was next. Nora wore two braids that went all the way down her back, and she bragged incessantly about her Beta tape collection. She had over 500 of them. I never believed her but it turned out it was true because I got to see them all on a shelf one time at a sleepover. Nora was the biggest brown-noser in our whole class and probably hadn't even listened to Anya because she was so busy preparing her list of questions.

"Nora?" Even Mrs. Barton looked annoyed.

"Yes, Anya. I was wondering if you could share with us what the role of Santa Claus is in the Swedish tradition." She pursed her lips and looked with fake-expectancy as I rolled my eyes and vowed to keep quiet so I could watch *Gremlins* at her house later.

Anya smiled.

Which was considerate of her, considering she was about to ruin my life.

"Well," she began, "when we all *still believed* there was a Santa Claus . . ."

Wait.

What?

WHAT?

She proceeded to tell the class that they used to believe he came and gave presents and all of that stuff but now they knew the truth and on and on and on.

I stared at her in disbelief, watching the clouds of smoke drift around her little crown where the candles had just been blown out.

I started to panic.

I looked at Mrs. Barton the same way I would look at a flight attendant on a really bumpy flight. Just trying to get my bearings and understand what an expert was thinking. She looked like she had swallowed a rat. Apparently they hadn't gone over this part in the dress rehearsal.

Cyril started crying and Mrs. Barton handed him an unlit candle.

There was a quiet mumbling throughout the class until finally the librarian told us it was time to go. On the way out, Anya handed me a weird bun thing and some candy and told me to have a Merry Christmas.

I looked at her with my mouth wide open, trying to form some kind of sentence that would restore order into my life.

"You lied in there, Anya. He is real. He *IS*." I couldn't help it—I started crying my eyes out. I walked down the rest of the hallway with a homemade Swedish bun in one hand and my innocence in the other.

As we rounded the corner, the other second grade class was eagerly waiting to enter the library and I caught eyes with a girl I had never seen before. She looked particularly excited and had on a sweater with a pair of real mittens sewn to the front. They were hideous. I considered starting with a fashion tip but decided to move past it because the line had started going.

"Don't go in there," I whispered to her.

Too late. They were on their way in and Anya already had her crown all lit up again.

"My name is Lucia . . ." I heard her start.

The girl glanced back at me as the big wooden door closed and I said a little prayer for her. It wasn't so much directed at God, because I was still a little irritated about letting that girl burn up just because she believed in Him. I didn't hear a word Mrs. Barton said for the rest of the day and I sat by myself in the cafeteria, trying to think through how I was going to broach the subject with my mom when I got back to our apartment.

It was a long day and a long taxi ride home.

My mother was sitting at the dinner table when I got home. She had already pulled out an after-school snack for my sister and me.

"Jennifer, go in your room." I pointed to her door, waited for her to walk in, and shut it behind her before I walked to my mother. She didn't need to know all of this yet. She had two years before one of Anya's sisters would spook out the class and destroy Christmas forever.

I sat on my mom's lap, buried my head in her sweater, and started crying again.

"He's not real, is he, Mommy?" I finally got out.

Her hand was stroking my hair and it stopped for a moment as she considered how to answer my question.

"Who told you that, Angela?"

I couldn't breathe and I gasped it out in pieces.

"It . . . was . . . *LUCIA!!!*" I sobbed.

The images of reindeer and elves flashed through my mind as I crumpled into her neck. She didn't say a word, and I knew.

It was all a lie.

He wasn't checking a list once, let alone twice.

He didn't have a wife or a house at the North Pole, and worst of all I had been sneaking my lunch to my sister for absolutely no good reason. All this work, for *NOTHING*.

I had wasted months, years even, and all that effort because I thought it mattered to someone.

I was reeling with disappointment, arms wrapped around my mother while I considered all I had once believed.

Fifteen minutes and three tissues later, I let my sister out of her room, wishing I could go back in time and play hooky from school that day.

I am an academic at heart. I like the facts, and I will take them with a side of evidence. I romanticize about things that add up, make sense, and can be proved true beyond a shadow of a doubt.

If I told you this was the basis of my relationship with Christ, or if I told you I had come to love Him by the process of elimination, I would be lying.

I'm also going to say something here that not many Christians want to say because they think it pokes holes in their testimony.

I have moments of doubt.

There. It's out on the table now.

Five words that threaten to convince everyone in the boat that I don't trust Him enough to get out and walk.

Do I believe Him? I do.

More than that, I have experienced Him in such a personal way that it would be hard to explain how I could ever doubt. And yet I do.

Either you just threw this book on the ground because you are convinced it's blasphemy or you are nodding in agreement as you consider your own stormy seasons. I'm going to guess the latter, mostly because if you did throw the book down then you probably didn't get to this sentence anyway.

See? Logic is my friend.

For years I saw myself as lesser than my Bible study counterparts who were raised believing and didn't understand how anyone could love God and doubt at the same time.

I don't think it's possible to live this life without room for doubt.

And even more shockingly, I don't think God holds it against us. After all, if He wanted us to know we could walk on water, I think He would have designed us to do it.

He doesn't need a bunch of robots wandering around the world telling everyone that if they really believed they wouldn't have moments of questioning.

I don't believe God is intimidated by our questions. In fact, I think He is pleased when we engage with Truth in such a way that questions result. It isn't like we're going to stump Him and see all of humanity unravel because we found the gap in His theater production. He isn't pacing through heaven, biting His nails, wondering if we will figure Him out and ruin the charade.

Instead, He is standing just outside the reach of our fingers, willing us to bridge the gap in faith.

Could He have ran to Peter, scooped him up, flew around the sky a few times and then plopped down on the boat with a giant, "TA-DA"?

He absolutely could have.

But where's the faith in that? And also, where is the bunny He's going to yank out of His hat for His next trick?

God isn't a magician who thrives on illusion and grandeur, pulling up audience members to assist Him in His routine.

He doesn't need us on stage in order to be God.

I want you to really soak this up, because as simplistic and familiar as it sounds, I genuinely believe it has the potential to change some of your thinking.

God will still be God if you stay in the boat.

But He won't be *your* God unless you get out.

And what you will find is probably similar to what I have found. I have great, beautiful strides of faith and then other times when the wind seems a formidable foe, and I buckle in the wake of what surrounds me.

And what if it's all a lie? What if we put our stock in the Jesus-Man and we realize it was a hoax? I don't believe this is the case, and I am willing to stake my life on it, but there are moments when the water is choking me and I wonder if I shouldn't have just put on a life vest and braved it out with the others.

And I'm not the only one.

Remember Thomas? *Doubting* Thomas?

I would say he was pretty straightforward about his questioning as he replied to the disciples who had seen the risen Christ.

"Unless I see the nail marks in his hands and put my finger where the nails were, and put my hand into his side, I will not believe it" (John 20:25).

Well then. This had to be the mother of all awkward silences.

I think there's another side of the coin, though, and one we should consider as believers.

Other people believing and telling you their story is powerful, but it isn't a substitute for experiencing it yourself.

More than a week passed and I imagine Thomas started to feel justified in his thinking. He may have been disappointed and perhaps he even tried to sway the others as he considered the overwhelming likelihood that Jesus the so-called Christ was dead and buried, never to be heard from again.

And then one day, despite the fact that the door was locked, Jesus entered the room and said to the group, "Peace be with you!" (John 20:26).

I stand corrected. Maybe there was a more awkward silence.

At this point He speaks only to Thomas, saying, "Put your finger here: see my hands. Reach out your hand and put it into my side. Stop doubting and believe" (John 20:27).

Chances are you have heard this story before, and you are thinking to yourself, "Well, sure. I wouldn't doubt Him either if He was standing right in front of me."

For years I have considered this passage, envious of those who got to touch His humanity and walk in total belief. But it wasn't until recently that I noticed something interesting about the story. We assume that Thomas touched Jesus and as a result he believed, but we aren't told that explicitly in the text. Nowhere in the account is there a moment where Thomas actually lays a hand on Him. Instead, we hear him exclaim, "My Lord and my God!"

I ask Him to reveal Himself to me in ways that would make Him impossible to doubt too.

In a sense, it's irrelevant if Thomas actually touched Him. More importantly, God provided the evidence to swallow the doubt. Thomas wanted to touch Him, and he said he wouldn't believe until he did. Maybe he did put his hands in the wound, but then again, maybe he didn't.

It's possible that he saw enough of the risen Lord to know that his way didn't matter anymore, and cried out in awe to the One Who stood before him.

Beauty and blessing don't come from our hands being in the evidence, but from the faith that comes from trusting Him *in spite of* the evidence.

Many times I have wondered to myself, "What if I die and find that all of this was nonsense and I believed for nothing? What if there is no eternal life?" It used to bother me when I considered the possibility, but I have gotten to a point of peace. After Audrey died I wanted reassurance that I would see her again and I couldn't help but wonder if it was all just wishful thinking. My life experiences say He is real and I am choosing to believe that one day I will have life with Him forever.

The book of John has been a sweet balm to me as I have experienced this particular fear. In fact, the word "believe" occurs 98 times in this Gospel alone, and the entire book emphasizes the deity of Christ. As we read John, we see the Lord perform miracles while professing His Sonship explicitly. John was not only the first disciple to believe that Jesus had risen from the dead, but also the first to recognize Him after His resurrection. In essence, the beauty of the Gospel of John is that he *believed*.

While I relate more to Peter, I love the way John loved his Savior. His words drip with devotion and passion for the Lord, and I find myself in awe of his unfailing faith. How do we get there? Well, I don't know that we necessarily have to.

We must have faith, yes. But to remove every single bit of doubt? Friend, not even those closest to Jesus Himself were able to accomplish this.

I can think of several times in my life when Satan wanted me to believe I wasn't really a believer, taunting me with images of people who never seemed to question. The more I pressed into Christ, the more clearly I saw Him. Was it perfect? No. But that's what made it so precious to me.

But what if I don't experience Him like others seem to?

This is going to sound like chastisement, but it isn't, I promise. It is me, coffee cup in one hand and the other wrapped around you in love. Hear these words and consider them in a way you may not have before.

If you have not seen Him the way others have, it may be because you are still in the boat, a mere observer to the miracles others have experienced.

I speak from experience.

I used to watch as He did incredible things for people around me, and I envied their relationship with Him. I would love to tell you that I saw an infomercial that walked me through the three-step program to get to know Him, or that I simply woke up one day and I believed.

Here's the hard part of what I want you to hear.

Hang on. Take a sip of coffee before I hit you over the head with this next part.

We are not called to be passive in our relationship with the Lord.

Is it possible that you doubt much because you are waiting instead of moving?

I'm not talking about enrolling in a class or volunteering at a homeless shelter because you know you are supposed to learn and live a sacrificial life.

No one who truly wants to know Christ and opens up their heart (and Bible) to Him will walk away empty-handed. That's a pretty bold claim for a 5'1" 98-pound girl (That last part is a lie. A beautiful lie, but a lie nonetheless.) to make, isn't it? Well, it isn't my claim to make . . . it is God's. He promises that His word will not return to Him empty (Isaiah 55:11), so I challenge you to read through the Scriptures with a heart that is seeking truth, inviting Him to reveal Himself as you go.

As a visual for your seasons of doubt, I want you to imagine the night that Peter called out to the Lord.

I like to see this moment in Scripture as a series of choices, and in each choice there is encouragement for those of us who struggle with fear.

First, we have the choice to either trust in God enough to start walking or stay in the boat. Hopefully we are obedient and get to see the Lord's power at work. We coast along, so happy to be doing what seemed impossible. But, like Peter, we can be distracted by what's around us. All of a sudden we lose eye contact and we realize how absurd it is to be doing something like this. Walking on water? Maybe this was a bad idea . . .

Peter didn't do as well with this choice, and instead of leaving his faith where he should have, he allowed his environment to dictate his response (sound familiar?).

At this point, he was panicked. The water is everywhere and he was trying to get his bearings. He realized he had a split second to make the next decision, and it's the one I love the best.

Now remember that Peter was in between a boat of men he can see and touch and the Man who claims He is the Son of God. Also remember that several of the disciples nearby were *fishermen*.

The water was their life, and surely they had come up against bad weather before, right? I imagine they weren't that far away from Peter. As I consider this image in my mind it leaves me breathless.

He is sinking between a boat of able-bodied men and the Man who claims to be the Son of God.

And guess what?

So are we.

Every single moment of every single day, we have to make this choice.

Them?

Or *Him.*

How many times have I relied on the men in the boat instead of my Lord?

Many.

Maybe they came in the form of a doctor, a friend, an expert. Someone who I can wrap my hands around and look in the eye. Someone who was predictable, knowledgeable, or strong.

I'm sinking; you've got to get out here and help me . . .

To me, what Peter did wasn't necessarily notable because he took his eyes off Jesus and lacked faith.

Did he doubt? Sure he did. And we might too.

But when push came to shove, *regardless of his fear in doing so,* Peter called out to Jesus instead of the men.

His life on the line, terrified and bewildered by his circumstances, he said only one name.

Lord.

This, my friends, is walking in a faith that transforms.

It's the voice crying out above the wind, in full knowledge of the fact that it doesn't necessarily add up from a worldly perspective.

Three words so easily overlooked, and yet they hold the key to a faith that challenges fear.

Lord, save me . . .

And what does our Jesus do in return?

"*Immediately* Jesus reached out his hand and caught him" (Matthew 14:31, emphasis mine).

He didn't rescue Peter when he started to sink.

He rescued him when Peter called to Him.

After catching him, He asks him this question: "You of little faith, why did you doubt?" (Matthew 14:31).

How do I answer that question in my life?

I must have read this story about fifty times before I realized that God wasn't chastising Peter for not having faith. Instead, He asks why he doubted, saying he had "little" faith. The Greek word here comes from the root word "*oligos*," and literally means "small." He isn't lacking in faith completely, it's just, well, small in this moment.

So while I don't think the Lord is unsympathetic to our fears, I also see something else here that I think is worth processing.

There was a walk of faith ahead of Peter that he will never know.

He got a glimpse of it, yes.

But I have to wonder . . . what would the rest of it have looked like? Did the Lord have something beautiful waiting and he missed it? In my heart, I see this as the intention of the Lord's heart as He questions Peter.

Why didn't you have enough faith to keep walking? I had such a great experience waiting for you if you would have just taken a few more steps. I don't want you to miss what I have for you in these times of trial, so stop doubting. Stop having a faith that gives up. Keep one foot in front of the other so you can see for yourself that I can do the impossible. Am I capable of rescuing you? Of course I am. But you could have had something different . . . something powerful . . . something you had to learn about Me for yourself . . .

Essentially, I think God doesn't want us to live life as near-drowning victims, calling out in desperation as we cling to life. This is not abundant life. As I read this story and consider myself in Peter's place, I know what it feels like to lose sight of Jesus. But I can't help but wonder as a reader what would have been.

We will see that in later days, Peter will deny Christ three times before He dies. As much as he loves the Lord, his love simply isn't strong enough to dictate his decisions in the face of great fear.

It pains me to think of what I might have done differently in my life if I had always kept my eyes on Him and battled my fear by simply taking one more step. There have been many missed opportunities, many supposed-failures, and much heartbreak over what I think the Lord could have done through just a little bit more belief on my part.

If we believe He made the waves to begin with (and I hope you do), we are fools to rely on the fishermen. And the walk we have ahead of us will shape every single storm we face for the rest of our lives. It will remind us that He is trustworthy, and that He has good mapped out for us.

I love this description of the passage we have been discussing:

> In these four contexts Jesus uses these two terms to define a faith that fails to grasp the opportunity for expression. It breaks down and needs fixing and restoration. Yet such failure can only happen, ironically, because these people have faith in Jesus. These words cannot apply to the Jewish religious leaders because they do not have any faith in Jesus at all. His disciples, conversely, have followed him and will continue to do so, even though they do not understand everything and often fail to exhibit the confidence and trust in Jesus that he deserves and desires.[4]

It is the same word that is used in the well-recited parable about the mustard seed, where Jesus says, "Because you have so little faith. I tell you the truth, if you have faith as small as a mustard seed, you can say to this mountain, 'Move from here to there' and it will move. Nothing will be impossible for you" (Matthew 17:20–21).

I can miss some of the blessedness that comes from a life of belief in the absence of proof.

I could miss the feeling of being pulled up out of the rushing water, His breath on my face urging me to remember His faithfulness.

In the words of Jesus Himself, "Blessed are those who have not seen and yet have believed" (John 20:29).

Where are you looking tonight? To the shore, so many miles away? To the boat full of men you trust? Or have you been gasping for air, convinced you can save yourself?

If so, I can understand your fear.

So unsteady, this life. So unpredictable and frightening.

I have been there and still fight it.

But I tell you this with the most sincere heart, longing for you to feel what I have felt when it seemed I wouldn't escape.

I just needed a mustard seed-sized faith in order to turn my head in the right direction, and as soon as He pulled my weight into His arms, I wondered myself . . .

Why, Lord?

Why did I ever doubt You?

I am going to take the Lord at His word, even if I have to do it on a minute-by-minute basis. You can too.

Lord, I do believe.

Help me overcome my disbelief that I may be blessed with intimate knowledge of Your power. Remind me daily that You are the

God who delights in our trust in You. Thank You, Lord, for the man who dared to walk in faith, and more than that, called Your name out in the midst of it all. He has taught me the beauty of choosing You, over and over again.

May Your name, and Yours only be the only One on my lips, in spite of the storm.

And maybe, just maybe . . .

Because of the storm.

Know that I pray these words over every person reading this book—that the Lord may bless you as you learn to trust the sound of His voice, and walk in the faith that brings a peace this world can never offer.

May the sea be good to you, but when it isn't, may you trust the One Who bids you, "Come . . ."

And walk, love.

CHAPTER 10

THE SCROLL OF REMEMBRANCE

FEAR OF GOD

Are we supposed to fear God?

I have read a lot of different translations of the Bible and more commentaries than I can count on all my fingers and toes, and I am here to tell you: yes.

I went into this book considering all of the things we shouldn't fear, praying I would encourage you in any areas with which you struggled, but now it's time to drop the big bomb.

We are called to fear God.

I'm going to try my best to simultaneously blend the fear of God with the knowledge that He is good, trustworthy, and able to make Himself small enough to feel like a friend.

That is kind of an awkward juxtaposition, however, so please be patient with me as I try to do so.

I have talked to a lot of people about what the "fear of God" is and while I'm still a long way from arriving at a complete understanding, it is starting to settle in my bones in the way that I believe it's supposed to.

When we think about fear, it doesn't sound like a good thing. Sure, there are times when it comes in handy in order to alert us to danger, but fear isn't typically associated with positive growth. So, when I say we should fear God, you may think of the way you have feared someone else in your life and the way that made you feel.

Many people—perhaps particularly women—say they feared their fathers growing up. They choke back tears as they recall what it was like to live in a home where Dad was unpredictable, vengeful, controlling, and so on. Or perhaps these adjectives describe another authority figure in your life. You can't help but want to distance these thoughts from your experience of God. It is hard to do that, though, and the God of the Bible feels especially distant in some cases, striking down people and destroying entire lands on what looks to us like a whim. We get tangled up in our emotional response to the idea of fear. We run from any opportunity to identify our God with those in life we have feared on this earth.

I had a wonderful, loving father growing up and I am so grateful to have a role model who shows me what a good, gracious man acts like. He made me feel safe and I always, always knew how much he loved me and would do anything for me.

With that said, I was still a little afraid of him.

Not afraid because I thought he would punish me when I didn't deserve it or that he would hurt me in his anger. Rather, I feared him because I knew that he was my superior and he had a right to discipline me when I had earned it. It didn't make him a bad father, but it did make me realize who I was in his presence.

I am not the rule-maker. I can certainly share my thoughts and requests and I can always rely on him, but at the end of the day, what he says goes.

Period.

So, as we proceed with a discussion of the fear of God, I want you to consider a person in your life who is like my dad is to me. Someone you respect, admire, and trust. Like I do with my dad, you fully recognize that you are not their equal and you respond to them with this in mind. For me, at least, this doesn't have the effect you might think.

If I didn't *trust* my father, it would be a nightmare to "fear" him, because I wouldn't have any way to determine whether or not what he was doing was really best for me. But I do trust him, and as much as I despised being banned from a certain friend's house or the way he insisted I be home at a certain time to avoid consequences, I know he had my best in mind.

Now that we have the right kind of earthly person in mind, let's clarify what is meant when we talk of "fear" in relation to God. Surely we aren't supposed to be terrified of Him, right? Many would say that the word "fear" really means "awe" or "reverence" when we are talking about the Lord. So I'm supposed to reverence Him, but not be terrified of Him, correct?

Well, a lot of folks say that and I believe there is truth in it. We are intended to live our lives in awe of who God is and the way He loves us, but I don't think that's the end of the story. (This next sentence might jolt you a little, but please stay tuned!)

I believe we should not only fear God in the sense that we revere Him, but also in the old "I am shaking in my boots in Your presence, God" kind of way. I think we make a huge mistake by not being afraid *enough* of God.

I have to admit that I'm someone who often comes to the Lord flippantly, and I catch myself so comfortable in His presence that it makes me feel, well, *uncomfortable*.

And if ever there comes a day when that discomfort subsides into ease, I will fear the outcome much more than I do now.

Should we fear the Lord?

Yes. Quite simply, without hesitation, we should.

But I'm not sure that we are supposed to be *afraid* of fearing God.

If you were here beside me I would watch your face to see if any of this was making sense in order to know where to go next. It is so important to me that you walk away from this chapter (and this book, for that matter) with the knowledge that you can trust God and you don't need to fear the life which fears God.

Let's go back to my dad for a minute (because he really likes these parts of my writing). Did I fear my father? I did. But it was in response to recognizing that he would hold me accountable for my actions. Ultimately, the fact that I feared him (as backwards as this might sound) was a safety net to me.

Years ago I read a book I loved called *Creative Correction* by Lisa Whelchel. In it she talks about how kids will test their boundaries, not so they can escape, but rather to determine how strong the fortress is. I love this analogy, and I see it in the flesh every day. My children rail against me, headstrong and determined to get the best of me but Todd and I (try to) respond with the consistency that reminds them that we are in charge. Truthfully, some of the hardest days we have together are those in which they see me failing to set boundaries. They don't like the feeling of swimming aimlessly around the house, doing whatever they please with no repercussions. Without necessarily recognizing it in the moment, they long for the love that says, *"That's far enough, love."*

Without that, they would get lost in the chaos. I am the voice that reminds them they aren't the bosses. Which is good, considering that they are in no position to run their own lives at this point.

And if I didn't feel the same way about myself, I suppose I would fear the "fear" of God. As it stands, I trust Him far too much (and myself far too little) to see it any differently than this:

The bigger He is to me, the smaller I must become. My favorite place to be is in the Hand of the God that whispers, "That's far enough, love."

Do you fear Him? I hope so. Because while it can be a scary thing to be so little in the bigness of God, it is far scarier to feel big enough to not need Him at all.

A necessary part of recognizing God is also accepting that we do well to tremble before Him. Not because we don't trust Him to do what is right, but rather because we *do*. None of us have it figured out, and none of us are perfect in our love for Him, but the goal should always be a solemn, glorious bowing of the knee that reminds us we are wholly reliant on His mercy in this moment and the next.

When you spend time in the Word of God and you have a relationship with Him, you are like the teenage girl who lies to her dad knowing that she stands in submission to someone who loves her enough to correct her. My knees should have been knocking together when I walked in that door (again, purely for example's sake) after telling my dad I was not *exactly* where I said I was going and there was a small chance that I had actually gone downtown instead. This (hypothetically) would have been problematic because I was explicitly told not to go downtown.

At this point, however, I had determined it would be the best thing to come out with it. Confess my transgressions with noble intent, fully submitting to whatever punishment he deemed appropriate.

Well, that, or I had a speeding ticket that had been issued to me outside a downtown club. (I am so creative at making up these totally hypothetical stories, aren't I? Ahem.) The evidence was stacked against me, and whether or not I wanted to admit it, I was in the wrong.

We live as sinners in a fallen world, where nothing we do can ever be worthy of the mercy we have received from God. Does that make you a little fearful? It should. Because you have a Father who desires to mold you until you more closely reflect Him to the rest of the world. The end goal here, folks, is not your glory. That kind of takes the wind out of the sails, doesn't it?

Well, it does unless you know the beauty of being hidden in His wounds, made to breathe His name in every opportunity you are given.

Scripture tells us that there are distinct blessings associated with fearing God. Among other things, He promises that those who fear will receive His blessing (Psalm 128:1), that they will have their desires met (Psalm 145:19), they will have strong confidence and a place of refuge (Proverbs 14:26–27), happiness (Proverbs 28:14), praise (Proverbs 31:30), and mercy (Luke 1:50).

The book of Proverbs is decidedly clear on the association of fear and wisdom. Over and over, the phrase "The fear of the LORD is the beginning of wisdom" occurs, and the heart of the book is summarized in those few words.

So what does this particular fear look like in our everyday life? Let's dissect this a little so that we have a good understanding of the original language and then we will apply what we have learned to our lives.

Proverbs 15:33 says, "The fear of the LORD teaches a man wisdom, and humility comes before honor." The word "teaches" is better translated as "is the instruction of," and is the same Hebrew word (*muwcar*) that is used in describing the correction of children by their parents. So when we fear the Lord, we could also say He instructs us. He has given us His rules for life throughout Scripture. Basically what we see throughout the book of Proverbs is the link between fear, obedience, and wisdom.

What is the evidence of our fear? Obedience.

What is the benefit of our obedience? Wisdom.

The fear of the Lord is the beginning of wisdom. When we fear Him the way we should, we stand in full recognition of His deity and authority over us. If we truly understand our position, we act in accordance with His commands.

I was scared to come home and tell my dad I had lied.

But apparently I wasn't too scared to disobey him in the first place.

This is where I believe the trembling comes in and the reason I fail to do so in the manner worthy of the King. I should be so fearful of disobedience that I don't do the thing He tells me not to.

The litmus test for our fear of God is pretty simple.

How well do you obey Him?

In light of the fact that we all find ourselves in the "less-than-perfect" boat, I would hasten to say your record could have been better. I know mine could have been (again, I'm just saying this as an illustration, okay?).

After I was grounded for a few weeks, my dad handed the keys back to me and told me I could go to a friend's house. He was very specific about the fact that this did not include (1) going downtown, (2) lying, and (3) a speeding ticket. I understood his request and I promised him I would do what he asked me to do.

I did.

And in an "I know the human example isn't the same as God but it serves as a good illustration" kind of way, I *practiced* fearing him.

And here's the cool part.

Later that night my dad sat me down and told me I could have a new car of my choosing and also that I no longer had a curfew.

Actually, that part really was hypothetical.

And if your expectation in fearing God is that you will be rewarded in the way you choose, let me give you a heads-up. You're probably going to be disappointed.

That is, unless you start to see that as your wisdom increases, so does your desire to please God. You will start to see (even if it's blurry) that what you see as punishment is actually a manner of teaching you to walk closer to Him. And as you move closer and closer, through many trials and temptations, you will find that true wisdom comes from aligning your will with God's.

You will experience the joy of knowing that you are living in accordance with what God Himself has deemed as best for you, and what you saw as setbacks will now take on a new life as blessings.

The more I fear God, the less I fear everything else.

I believe that true peace and true healing come from wisdom. Which comes from obedience. Which comes from, you guessed it, fear of the Lord.

This is why we shouldn't fear fearing when it comes to God.

Because the place of "God-shaped" fear holds the opportunity to walk in the way He has instructed us and only as we do that are we able to live a life blessed with His divine wisdom. And that wisdom is beautiful, life-giving, peace-ordaining, faith-filled journeying that doesn't worry about tomorrow. I've spent so much time trying to do God's job for Him that at times I have actually started to believe I can.

Now, to the best of my ability, I try to walk in light of my own smallness, because it illuminates the safety of His bigness.

Fear God in the way that makes your knees bend and your heart race. Reverence Him. Be in awe of who He is. Know that in His divine wisdom, He chose you, your circumstances, and every last hair on your head in order to woo you to trust and glorify Him the way He deserves to be glorified. He didn't choose you because of anything in you, but because of everything in Him.

Every single moment of your life is ripe with the opportunity to bless Him by taking Him at His word.

Beautiful trembling.

Awe-inspired fear.

Mike Yaconelli said the following, and I think it is a spectacular summary of my own thoughts on the fear of God.

> I would like to suggest that the Church become a place of terror again; a place where God continually has to tell us, "Fear not"; a place where our relationship with God is not a simple belief or doctrine or theology, it is God's burning presence in our lives. I am suggesting that the tame God of relevance be replaced by the God whose very presence shatters our egos into dust, burns our sin into ashes, and strips us naked to reveal the real person within. The Church needs to become a gloriously dangerous place where nothing is safe in God's presence except us. Nothing—including our plans, our agendas, our priorities, our politics, our money, our security, our comfort, our possessions, our needs . . . Our world is tired of people whose God is tame. It is longing to see people whose God is big and holy and frightening and gentle and tender . . . and ours; a God whose love frightens us into His strong and powerful arms where He longs to whisper those terrifying words, "I love you."[5]

Several years ago I had a really interesting conversation with my mother-in-law about the book of Malachi; specifically, the third chapter, where it says:

> "Then those who feared the LORD talked with each other, and the LORD listened and heard. A scroll of remembrance was written in his presence

concerning those who feared the LORD and honored his name." (Malachi 3:16)

She told me she loved the idea that there was a record of the way they "remembered" the Lord, and the fact that it was important enough to God that He took the time to notate it. In the book of Revelation we are told that there are "books" opened as the dead are judged (20:12), and she wondered if this was one of the books referenced. We don't know what they are for certain because Scripture doesn't identify any of them by name (with the exception of the book of life) but I agreed with her that it was an amazing image. A giant scrapbook of sorts, including all the moments in our life that we remembered the Lord, or deliberately chose to recognize Him.

I love that visual because it encourages me to make the conscious decision to remember. I think there are a couple other interesting things about this particular verse, namely that these were people who feared the Lord. We need to remember that the book of Malachi was written in a time when the Israelites were living lives that did not honor God. Essentially, most of the people had stopped concerning themselves with the consequences of sin and were just doing whatever they wanted. There was obviously a group of people who chose not to go with the masses, and encouraged one another in their desire to live holy lives in light of their fear of God. I love that they got together and made a point of talking with one another about their convictions. There is still a lot of wisdom in choosing to surround ourselves with people who also fear God and will hold us accountable and encourage us as we try to do the same.

The circumstances are different, but we, too, live in a society where we have become so self-sufficient that we don't always feel like we need God to sustain us.

It is so crucial that we have a group of people we can count on to remind us of our need for God. We get so caught up in what the world can do for us that we start to think we can do it on our own, and the greatest tragedies of life come when we turn from Him and rely on ourselves. It is an amazing gift to be able to fear the God who truly has the ability to change our circumstances. With that said, we need to be ever mindful of the fact that He is not a tame lion, and really believing that results in action. Period. If you have people around you who will allow you to walk in the opposite direction of God's commandments without confrontation, I suggest you find some that can love you better. That goes for us as observers too; if we are in the presence of sin and we don't act, then we need to consider our own hearts as well.

I hope I am always astounded that the Lord gives me the opportunity to come to Him.

So we have shared several hours together at this point, and you know quite a bit about my story. I hope that what you have seen is that you aren't alone in your fears, and you aren't a bad person because of them. I so desperately want to be able to write a summary chapter, a conclusion that lays it all out and gives you the solution that will replace your fear with faith. I have heard that so many times . . . trade your fear for faith . . . and yes, I do believe faith replaces fear. But I guess, in my mind, it just isn't as black and white as some people have made it sound. It is more of a balancing act, where we deliberately lean into Him and away from our fear.

If you feel like you cannot serve God truly until you stop fearing completely, you will miss opportunities around every corner. If you are convinced that God can't use a warrior who doesn't have any armor, or a man who doesn't have the skills to speak, or a woman who knows she has sinned, a man who ran in the opposite direction of God's calling, or even a woman who longed for her husband to love her more than her sister . . .

Let me take a moment to remind you, and I pray that these words will ring in your ears when you feel like you are washed up, overwhelmed and out of chances.

Yes, there was a snake.

And he delighted in proposing that God might not be enough.

But there is also a God who provides a staff, a whale, an army, a wrestling match, a baby, a wound fresh with blood to allow us to ask the questions that we may have shied away from for years.

Who is this Man, really?

He is the One Who bent low to the ground, hand moving and not saying a word while the crowds scattered and silence fell.

Because of *you*.

He is the One Who stopped walking on a crowded street because He wanted you to know that He knew your name and He knew your need.

He is the One Who watched the sky grow dark as His mortal life surrendered, because He wanted you to love Him with all of your days.

Do I fear?

Yes.

Do I love Him?

All the more.

Don't let your fear convince you that Love isn't bigger. Treasure the moments you see His favor and His mercy, and when you fear (and you will), remember that we need only have the fear that comes inexplicably wound to the love we have for Him. It isn't an easy trade, and it isn't a one-time deal, but when you have learned the joy in trusting, you will love the Lord in a way you never have before, I promise.

I will never forget a night many, many years ago when I was still living in Japan. I was terrified of storms, and I stared at the huge dark clouds hanging above our car as we drove to my teacher's house for supper. I asked my dad a bunch of questions and when we got there I ran into the hall closet and started crying. My teacher's wife found me and asked me to come out and talk to her for a few minutes. She also taught at my school and I always thought she seemed like a nice lady.

She sat beside me and pulled the curtains back on the window next to us.

I cringed as the lightning flashed.

"Angela, you know what?" She tapped the window with her fingernail.

I shook my head side to side, eyes filled with tears.

"I used to be really afraid of storms when I was a little girl." She took her finger from the windowpane and moved the hair away from my face. I didn't say anything but I was curious about what she might tell me next.

"And one day," she began, "when I was about your age, I figured out the trick. And guess what? I'm not scared of them anymore. In fact, I love them."

I had a feeling I was about to be shipped off somewhere so they could perform the same magic on me. It would probably be cheaper than my after-school counseling sessions.

I saw her hand start to move toward the window again and I couldn't believe my eyes. In one quick motion she turned the lock, flung the window wide into the night, and whispered, "You just have to open the window . . ."

I was paralyzed with fear and blinking my eyes faster and faster to try and get the rain out. I felt it hit my hands and my cheeks and I thought I was going to cry harder but I didn't. I realized I was holding my breath and I let it out in tiny pants, one after another, praying she would close it again.

Slowly, gently, and with more conviction than a Sunday morning, she took my clenched hand and reached it as far out the window as it would go.

"Open it, Angela. Trust me."

I watched my hand open as the goose bumps rose up on my arms, cold from the rain, and I couldn't help but smile at my own courage. She was still holding onto my hand, but as soon as I opened my fingers she pulled hers back.

"You aren't going to be afraid of it anymore. And you will always remember this moment and every one that comes to you in the future where you have the chance to learn to be brave." She had this happy glow on her face and she smiled at me, no doubt remembering some of her courageous moments.

I held my hand in the rain for at least five minutes as it fell onto the carpet, the top of my arm, and eventually, into my mouth as I leaned out the window, face toward the sky.

I promised her I would never forget, and I have stayed true to my word.

A few years ago I sat in front of a blank computer screen and I watched the cursor blink as I tried to decide if I should share my story. I was terrified and I couldn't bear the thought that I was pregnant with a baby who wouldn't survive.

I started typing, and I poured out my heart to the empty page. I pushed send and I settled into so many of my fears, wondering what people would say, what would happen to my daughter, my marriage, my heart . . .

I realized the computer was prompting me for a title. I smiled and let my fingers finish while a smile from a night so long ago crossed my mind and made me braver than I thought I could be.

"Bring the rain . . ."

Three words that have not only been the name of my blog, but the cry of my heart. And when I met my daughter I knew I had felt the warmth of a summer storm, brushing the eternal against my skin.

If you have heard me say only one thing in all this time, I pray it is this:

You have a God who longs to be the peace of your life and the glory of your days. He desires your relationship, your trust, and your obedience. He doesn't want you to live a life of fear, but the only way you will really believe Him is to do the thing that seems impossible.

It is pouring rain out there, and I know what your first thought is. I have been there myself, only I'm so glad I didn't stay. My prayer is that as you close this book, you will take a chance on the Savior of your soul, and let Him do what only He can.

Open the window, close your eyes, and let mercy wash you clean.

ACKNOWLEDGMENTS

Todd, Ellie, Abby, Kate, and Charlotte: I am so grateful I get to share life with you all. You have filled me with joy and given me a new love for Jesus. I pray that God will help me be the kind of wife and mother that make you each want to chase after Him. Thank you for your patience while I was writing and for your encouragement when I needed it. I love you all to the moon and back (a few times!)

Audrey: You will always be the inspiration for my writing and my speaking. I want your name to be in every page of thank-you's I ever write, despite the fact that I know you are in a place where these pages pale in comparison to the love only a Father could give you. I can't wait to see you, sweet girl. One day I will tell you face to face how you made me brave, but until then, know we love you and miss you every single day.

Mom and Dad: Your love and support of me has led me to believe I can do something crazy like write a book or stand up in front of people and share my life. I don't know where I would be without your wisdom, dedication, and passion for anything I ever wanted to do. I have never known parents more enthusiastic and proud, and I love you both so much.

Grandma: I wrote about you a little in this book, but a whole book couldn't hold all the things I love about you. I am so grateful that my kids get to experience you in their childhood the same way I did, with lots of cookies and Shirley Temple movies. You are such an amazing woman, and you have filled my life with memories and happiness. I love you so, so much grandma!

The Carter family: Jenn, Brian and Tuck-Jenn, I still smile when I think of all the times you were, umm, less than afraid of life than I was. I think we both remember a certain plane ride where you added a musical overture to my experience . . . You are so much fun and I am honored to be your sis. I love you, Brian and Tuck so much.

The Smith family: Mom and Dad Smith, The Sponberg's, The Smith's, and the Lantz family—you have each made such significant contributions to my walk with the Lord and have been instrumental in loving my family well. I love you all!

Audra: Thank you for your constant, enduring friendship and for the way you love me and my whole family. All my love to Shawn, Amelia and Aliza as well!

Jess (and Matthew): Jess, you are one of the most faithful people I have ever met, and loyal beyond words. I love you all dearly (And that includes you Elias!!! And pretty soon, Adeline!!)

Dan: You are the best friend a girl could have ever inherited through marriage. You make life fun, and we treasure your wisdom, your heart, your love for our girls, and your unwavering devotion to the Lord. We love you so much and appreciate all of the sacrifices you have made for us, and we are so happy that every year we get weeks of time with you to play cards, sit on the beach, and laugh our heads off. Thank you for everything you are to us, Dan.

Kelsey: We are so grateful that God gave us to you right in the season we needed you most! You have survived a flood, a birth, a broken arm, tornado warnings, birthdays, holidays, speaking engagements that shall remain nameless, and so much more. You've seen the worst of us and love us all in spite of it!!! We all love you so much!!!

For Pete, Brandi, Blake, Ally and all of our Crosspoint friends and family, we are so grateful to have a church home that knows how to do the hard, beautiful work of the gospel. Thank you for supporting us and being a city on a hill-we love you all so much.

Greg (Daniel): I am so grateful that God saw an opportunity for us to work together. I so enjoy having you on my team, and greatly appreciate your wisdom and desire to support me in the best way possible. Thank you so much for all of your hard work and for believing in the girl you just sat down with for Starbucks.

Thank you to B&H who has loved and supported me through the loss of my daughter, and who has faithfully shown me what love should look like when business and creativity collide. You have set the bar very high, and I am grateful beyond words that you have allowed me to be a part of your team.

Jennifer: I have never known anyone to be as supportive, enthusiastic, and dedicated as you. Of all the compliments and accolades I could bestow upon you (and there are more than would fit in my page count). I think the best one is simply the way you have loved my Audrey girl. From the very beginning and every day since then, you have been and faithful editor and more than that, a close friend. I thank God constantly for allowing me the blessing of working with you, knowing that you always have my best in mind and also that you know the best places to waste time in an airport. I cannot imagine having gone through the past several years without you on my team; everything that is hard, scary, overwhelming, hidden, tearful, broken in me . . . you make it beautiful. You are such a gift, Jen. I love you very, very much.

Thank you, Lord for allowing me to do what I love. Thank you for everything You did on my behalf, and the way You have carried me through all the seasons I have walked. I pray that any offering I have in Your name will be worthy of the calling You have given me, and that I will share you unashamedly at every opportunity. It is only by Your grace that these pages have come into existence, and I don't take a moment of it for granted. I love You, Lord. Sola gratia . . .

NOTES

1. See http://www.kesertorah.org/mastering_fear.pdf.

2. Matthew Henry, *Concise Commentary on the Bible*, "Hebrews 2." See www.biblegateway.com.

3. Some scholars debate the exact historical and biblical placement of this story as it is not in some of the earliest copies of John's Gospel. However, all agree that the teaching we glean from this account is consistent with the whole of biblical teaching and Jesus' earthly ministry as well as the reality that there is sufficient evidence that an account such as this did occur in Jesus' ministry. If you are interested in studying more about this passage's placement in Scripture and a deeper view of how to understand and apply God's Word, I suggest John Piper's sermon on this text to be found at http://www.desiringgod.org/resource-library/sermons/neither-do-i-condemn-you—3.

4. See http://moments.nbseminary.com/archives/fixing-a-broken-faithologopistos-in-matthews-gospel.

5. See http://www.youthspecialties.com/articles/the-safety-of-fear.

AUTHOR INTERVIEW

WITH ANGIE SMITH

1. Your first book, *I Will Carry You*, chronicles the story and grace of the life of your daughter Audrey, who lived only a few hours. It's obviously a personal message, although the lessons learned and teaching elements are very strong. How has writing on something a bit more removed from your story been a different process?

I think it's the perfect follow-up book to *I Will Carry You*, because it is based on another subject that is really personal to me, but I think more people can relate to it. When I began writing I wasn't expecting it to be as emotional as it was, but it some sense it is a continuation of what I have learned in my walk with God in the wake of losing my daughter. I think any mom would say that one of her greatest fears is losing a child, so to have walked through that with the Lord has carved out a new depth in my relationship with Him and as a result, has influenced my idea of what fear really is. My prayer is that some of the things I have learned along the way will inspire others to move away from the kind of fear that steals our joy and threatens the hope we have in Christ.

2. You write in *What Women Fear* about the grip fear has had on you at different times in your life. Do you believe that fear is something we need to (or can) totally eradicate from our lives?

I started to write a long answer to this question because I think it is really interesting, but I think I'll stick with the bottom line. No. I don't. I don't think we can and I don't believe we need to. I'm not talking about the kind of fear that swallows you up and spits you out here, and I think it's worth noting the difference between crippling fear and the kind of fear that spurs us on to (good) action. As I read Scripture while writing, I was blown away by the way the Lord has used people's fears and made them into something beautiful.

3. How has your faith in Christ given you strength to fight fear? Can you give an everyday example of what this looks like lived out?

I think for all of us, it's a conscious choice to choose Him in all circumstances. We have to evaluate the situation, remember who God is in it, and rest in the promise that He has our best in mind. At the heart of dealing with fear is the relationship you have with God; the relationship has to trickle into every part of your life, filling the gaping hole of fear with the faith that releases us. One of my favorite chapters in the book deals with a story from Scripture where I feel like someone had to make a choice between faith and fear, and His response brought me to tears. It reminded me of my own humanity, but also the choice I get to make in moments where I feel hopeless.

4. Of all the fears you discuss in the book, which do you see most prevalently in the lives of the women around you or to whom you minister?

It's interesting because when you think about the word fear, you immediately process things that are dangerous in nature, of more phobia-type status. But when I actually asked women what they were afraid of, the answers were more everyday and social in nature. A lot of people say they are afraid of failing, afraid of being "found out," afraid of being abandoned or alone. It was reassuring to me that there were so many common threads, because I felt like it would touch those who didn't realize so many others had the same struggles.

5. You've been a writer for years and have a very popular blog but are now about to begin speaking at some very large conferences. How do you hope to see this message of transforming fears into faith take hold in that setting?

For me, just getting up there requires a tremendous leap of faith for me because it's terrifying! But I guess if I'm going to write a book on fears I need to get on out there and stand up to them, huh? Truthfully, what this chapter of my life represents is another chapter in the story of my life as a girl who has missed out on life because of my fears. It's a constant balance, a perpetual choice, but it's one of which I have seen the other side. I know what it's like to be caught by the arms of God and I want to live a life that shows others that it's a beautiful place to be.

"This is a beautiful and tender book that would touch any woman's heart, no matter her age or realm of experience. It is about a relationship so intimate with God that it carves a safe place for crisis of faith, for faith proved genuine and for divine callings willed, sealed, and fulfilled. Yes, this is one mother's moving story. This one mother also happens to be a true writer. We will hear more from her."
—Beth Moore on *I Will Carry You*

ALSO FROM
ANGIE SMITH

I Will Carry You
The Sacred Dance of Grief and Joy

Chapter 1 Sampler

Chapter 1
Us

And the cup he brings, though it burn your lips,
has been fashioned of the clay which the Potter
has moistened with His own sacred tears.
—Kahlil Gibran[*]

If there is one thing I have learned about raising three daughters, it is this: it is an unspoken law that if you are running late, you will not be able to find the sixth shoe.

It's life as a mommy. They are running in every direction, full of life: and all the while you are trying to rein them in and explain why Mrs. Adams won't understand if we are late for gymnastics again. Most of the time I just giggled and chased them around until I inevitably caved and let them wear mismatched shoes, imagining the looks of horror I would receive from the on-time moms.

Our biggest problems in life during the girls' younger years were things like finding the sixth shoe.

[*] I have been encouraged and ministered to by the words of various writers as I've gone through the grieving process. I am so thankful for the way the Lord has used their words in my life. However, quoting specific words from any author should not be understood to be an endorsement or sign of agreement with everything they have written.

I miss those days.

We made plans for forever, like you're supposed to do when you're a family. We were so in love with our life that it was impossible to consider anything else. Just love one another deeply and try to make each moment count for something. Run the race with joy, and it will all be OK.

How could we have known?

And even if we had, I can't say we would have done it any differently. We loved without abandon, each day and night filled with the hope and expectation that we would always be together. Whether nestled under a cozy quilt watching a movie or photographing the girls having a hose fight with the neighbor kids in the backyard, one thing was for sure . . .

We were a family, and everything was exactly as it should be.

My husband Todd sings in a Christian group called Selah, and when I look back at the way God started our family, I can't help but wonder how we managed to keep our sanity.

Just a few months after we were married, I was right in the middle of a conversation with Todd when it happened. I don't remember what we were talking about, but I do know I made a rather abrupt exit as I dashed to the bathroom with my hand over my mouth. I spent the next few hours assuming I had a nasty flu, but in the morning I realized the timing of this "flu" was a little suspicious. Todd ran to the store and bought our first of many pregnancy tests, and I watched as the little line told me I was going to be a mommy. We were completely shocked, but after about six more tests (anyone else done this?) with the same result, I figured it was really happening. I stared in the mirror as I got ready to go out that day, looking at my reflection and imagining what it was going to look like in the coming days.

I never got the chance to see that.

At around nine weeks I miscarried the baby, and I was devastated. Todd was sad, but he hadn't connected the way I had with the baby. His biggest concern was making sure I was OK. He was so tender with me as I tried to process the fact that there had been a life inside me that was gone.

That was the first time in our marriage that we had to walk through loss. We knew it wouldn't be our last, and that our vows included times like these, but it was hard. As a woman, I wondered if something was wrong with me. I would stay awake at night and wonder if I would ever have children. I had just finished a graduate degree in developmental psychology, and pretty much every decision I had made in my life revolved around my love for children. I couldn't help but wonder if motherhood wasn't going to happen the way I had always dreamed it would.

We were fortunate that the Lord didn't wait long to bless us again. I will never forget being out on the road with Todd, sensing that something was happening. It was eleven at night and I told him we needed to find a store that was open so I could take a pregnancy test. He covered his head with a pillow and laughed (mostly because I said this every month in the hopes that it would come up with the pretty pink line).

"Todd. We're in Maryland. You know how I am with finding my way around. What if I get lost?" He looked up at me with tired eyes, pleading with me to let it go.

"Honey, can we go in the morning? Let's get some sleep, and we can do it on the way out."

Clearly he did not understand the urgency of a woman in this mind-set.

"No, I can't wait. I have got to go now. There has to be something right around the corner." I grabbed the rental car keys and kissed him on the forehead.

He fell back on to the bed, knowing I wasn't going to budge.

"And Toddy? You are seriously going to regret not going with me if it turns out I'm pregnant." I smiled mischievously and closed the door behind me while he laughed.

I came back into the hotel room about a half hour later and ran straight for the bathroom. I watched as the colors changed immediately, clue number one to what we would later discover. Without even bothering to wait for it to make it all the way across the little screen, I opened the bathroom door and held the stick straight in front of me. I waited a second to make sure he was paying attention and then peeked my head out with a giant smile.

Todd sat straight up in bed, his eyes adjusting to the light and his mind adjusting to what was happening.

"Are you serious?"

I nodded.

I screamed with delight and jumped into bed, settling into my familiar spot on his chest.

He grabbed the test and stared at his future.

"Congratulations, Daddy."

In disbelief he set his hands on my stomach.

"Wow." It was about all he could manage.

"Yeah, wow."

We lay in silence for a few minutes, smiling in the darkness.

"Hey babe?" I asked.

"Yeah?"

"You totally should have come with me."

We laughed as we pulled the covers up, both of us in awe that God had chosen us.

And boy, had He ever.

After my initial miscarriage I had gone to the library down the street and checked out a book about pregnancy loss. The sweet librarian recognized me and acknowledged my pain as she scanned the book.

"God bless you, honey." She looked deep into my red eyes, ministering to me without another word.

I started to cry because it was such a simple gesture, and it meant more to me than I knew how to say to her.

After I got the positive test result, I was eager to go back and check out another book—this time, one on pregnancy. I saw the librarian working at the counter and waved. A few minutes later I set down three pregnancy books on the counter, and she clapped her hands in delight.

A few days later I went in for my twelve-week checkup, and they did an ultrasound.

After a rather shocking appointment, I made my way back to the library and smiled when I saw my library friend working. I watched her face light up as I set down a new set of books.

This time they were on parenting *twins*.

She looked up at me in total shock and started laughing.

"Oh, God bless you, honey! I'm sort of hopin' for your sake that I won't be seein' you tomorrow!"

Aside from some discomfort, everything seemed to be going smoothly with my pregnancy, but my doctor suggested I have another ultrasound at around twenty-five weeks just to make sure. We knew we were having two girls and we were pretty set on names. At the end of August, we went in to have another look at the babies, and within about a minute we knew something was terribly wrong. The technician who was doing the ultrasound looked like he was in shock, and he got tears in his eyes as he told us he needed to get his supervisor. I felt like I couldn't breathe, and I asked him if they were alive.

"They are alive right now."

Those words will haunt me for the rest of my life.

His supervisor explained that I was dilated about three and a half centimeters, and that my body was threatening to go into labor. She told me I needed to get right to the hospital, and they called for a wheelchair as they weren't even comfortable with letting me stand up.

I sobbed the whole way over. My first night in the hospital a sweet nurse came in and sat with me, explaining that my babies were on "the cusp of viability," and that they were going to do everything they could to keep them inside me for as many weeks as possible. She was incredibly kind but also honest, and the truth was that it was an incredibly serious and unpredictable situation. A few days later I had surgery to try to prevent my cervix from opening any more. I continued to be on a round of the most horrific drugs known to man.

If you are familiar with magnesium sulfate, you understand. They had me on that one for three weeks. At one point I thought my IV pole was a trick-or-treater. Todd was on the road, and my best friend Audra was with me, so at that point she told me she thought it would be a good idea to go to sleep.

After ten weeks of touch-and-go in the hospital, they felt I was in a safe zone and sent me home. They stopped one of my medications a few days later, and I started having contractions. I had a gloriously short and easy delivery, and on December 2, 2002, we welcomed Ellie and Abby into the world just two minutes apart. Weighing in at four pounds eleven ounces and three pounds eleven ounces respectively, they were tiny but perfect.

Abby was rushed to the NICU immediately, and we never heard her make a sound. She had a few complications with her breathing, but overall she did great. She was an itty-bitty thing, but she was a fighter!

We brought Ellie home from the hospital, set down her baby carrier, and I kissed Todd good-bye as he left for his Christmas tour. I will never forget those first few moments of silence after the door closed behind him. I stared at Ellie in her car seat and just began to weep. I was hormonal, alone, and in charge of two people's lives. I was scared stiff. I had one baby at home and the other in the NICU, and trying to nurse two babies on different schedules who were a half an hour away from each other was, to say the least, very difficult.

One night, when I felt like I had reached the end of myself, I walked into the NICU and heard a familiar sound. It took me a minute to put it together, and when I did, I asked what they were listening to. The nurse (who had no idea who my husband was) replied, "It's the new Selah Christmas CD, and it is so, so great."

I couldn't believe it.

"Do you listen to it a lot?" I asked.

Tears filled my eyes as I anticipated her answer.

"Oh yes, all the time. The babies love it."

I started crying because all this time, when I felt awful that Todd and I couldn't be there with her every moment, God had provided a way for her daddy to be singing over her. The nurses came to me and put their arms around me as I told them who I was and why this CD was so special to me. I remember one of the ladies reminding me that His ways are not our ways and we must believe even when we can't see the way out.

Abby made such great strides that our prayers were answered, and she came home just before Christmas. The high-risk doctor who treated me came into my room one day and, in a hushed tone, told me that my God had performed a miracle. He smiled as he left the room, and at that moment I had no idea that I would see him again a few years down the road in a much different situation.

Lights strung, presents wrapped, and two redheaded bundles that had defied the odds. Could life get any better? In the midst of it all, Todd and I fell in love with each other in a whole new way. We stayed up late at night and played cards in bed, covering each other's mouths to stifle laughter that might wake the babies. We realized the awesome responsibility we had been given and dove into it headfirst.

The peace of God settled into our tiny apartment every night as Todd sang lullabies and I gently rocked the girls to sleep. After sneaking out of their room (which was a closet!), we would play rock-paper-scissors to see who would feed which baby during the night.

The loser had to take Abby, who was notorious for waking up at least ten times during the night. When I would hear her stirring at 4:00 a.m., I would tickle Todd tauntingly and whisper, *"Your baby's up, hon. Have fun!"* He would roll over and whack me with a pillow. The next night we reversed roles. When I think about that time in our lives, I just remember laughter. I really understood what love was supposed to be and who I wanted to be as a mother. We were sleep deprived for sure, but we couldn't get enough of them. We lived in a hazy blur of joy and chaos, knowing that above all we were really in it together now.

A few months later I was dancing with Todd at a friend's wedding, his scruffy cheek pressed against mine as we swayed together in an unspoken promise: *This will never be taken from us.*

We came home from the wedding and ran up to see our sleeping beauties, sweaty headed and flushed with the joy of another full day. Their personalities were starting to take shape, and since we loved Louis Armstrong's "What a Wonderful World," we dubbed the pensive Ellie our "dark sacred night," and gregarious Abby our "bright blessed day." I tucked them deep into the safety of their covers, and the same implicit promise filled the room: *This will always be ours.*

What a wonderful world indeed.

What can I say? The twins were pretty much the perfect kids. They slept all the time, they ate whatever we fed them, they were even tempered, they smiled at strangers, and loved to snuggle. They were

the kind of kids people fall in love with the moment they meet them. They wanted to help with everything around the house, cleaned up after themselves, played nicely with all their little friends, and constantly filled the house with the sound of joy.

I began to formulate a theory in my mind, which was based almost entirely on the fact that I must be the most perfect mother to ever grace the face of the earth. I smiled as people marveled at them sitting in the grocery carts while I shopped, and inwardly shook my head as we passed women with their unruly children. I nodded like royalty as women commented that they had never seen such well-behaved, sweet children. *Oh, why thank you. Really? Well, I guess we are just blessed to have such good girls. . . . You are too kind. . . . Oh, how sweet. . . .*

I have an image of God sitting in heaven, munching on a big bowl of popcorn as the days counted down to September 7, 2005.

It was a perfectly planned (see where this is going?), crisp, fall after-noon when Sarah Katherine Smith came raging into the world about an hour and a half after I went into labor (yes, you read that cor-rectly). She screamed like a wild animal in pain when they bathed her, smacked her way out of her newborn blanket, and stared at me with a look that said, "I'm going to need some more information here, lady." I heard a nurse make a comment under her breath about how I was going to have my hands full. I was not at all intimidated.

Clearly, I thought, *they did not know they were dealing with super mom.*

A few months passed, and I realized that the Lord, in His infinite (and often humorous) wisdom, had decided to give me the childhood version of myself to parent. I must say that the level of glowing sat-isfaction I have seen on my father's face in the past four years has approached sinful.

Kate is the most life-filled, passionate, willful blessing I have ever had the pleasure of raising. We always prayed that we would have a third child who wouldn't slip into the background and be overshadowed by the twins. When I was pregnant with her, I had horrible images of her sitting alone in the corner and feeling like a loner because she didn't have a partner the way they did. We prayed for her to have a voice, to have courage, to have strength, unwaver-ing enthusiasm, determination, and conviction. In retrospect I think we may have overdone it a little.

Her enormous brown eyes and deep husky voice bring life into every room she enters. I see a lot of myself in her. You can't keep that girl from what she wants; one day, when she gets her arms

around Jesus, she is going to take the world by storm. Until that day, I am drinking a lot of soothing tea and praying that I enter my late thirties with most of my hair.

When Kate was about two, we started talking about having another baby.

Let me restate that.

We had half a conversation and the stick turned pink.

Even from the beginning there was no question that this baby was supposed to be ours. We broke the news to the girls, who proceeded to request a boy who would not be interested in their toys. We told them we would do the best we could.

At about sixteen weeks we went in for a regular ultrasound, and we discovered that we were, much to the girl's chagrin, going to have another pair of sweet little girl hands digging in the Barbie bin. Other than that it was a normal ultrasound, although we did find out later that the technician had noted that there was less fluid than would be expected.

They suggested I have a follow-up ultrasound at around eighteen weeks just to make sure everything looked OK. We headed home with the thought that everything seemed to be all right. I had felt uneasy about this pregnancy from the beginning so it was nice to have a little reassurance. After my experience with Abby and Ellie, it was hard to ever feel totally at peace about being pregnant, but this was different. I felt so uneasy that I had trouble sleeping, and I Googled myself into every possible tragedy.

The kids actually took the gender announcement surprisingly well, and we moved into full swing nesting mode as a family. We took out one of the old cribs and set it up in Kate's room, which she was very pleased about because it meant graduation to a big-girl bed. We talked about names and all the fun things we were going to do with the new baby, and we stared at her ultrasound picture and dreamed of what life would be like with another car seat.

We decided to name her Audrey Caroline after my best friend Audra, with her middle name coming from mine (Carole). The girls were disappointed that we had eliminated "Shimmer," "Rainbow

Flurry," and "Feather Dancer" so quickly. Thankfully they approved of Audrey, so it was agreed.

We were going to have another stocking hanging from the mantle next year.

One of my tests came back slightly abnormal, but my doctor wasn't worried because this particular test has an extremely high rate of false positives. He did suggest that I go ahead and have a follow-up ultrasound to see if the baby had Down syndrome. As someone who has worked with this population of children, I wasn't intimidated by the possibility of a special-needs child, but I did want to know so that I could start preparing the children and making every effort to make sure Todd and I were educated.

I was a little nervous about the ultrasound, because as mothers we can't help but imagine the worst-case scenario. I tried to keep myself calm, reminding myself that the Lord had our best interest in mind. He knew what we could handle, and we had to have faith in that. Still, I was uneasy about the appointment; I feared it was more serious than we were anticipating.

My mother-in-law was in town and sensed the Lord told her to stay with me for my appointment so she canceled her flight and decided to come with us. As we sat in the waiting room, we tried to make small talk, but we were so distracted. Something just wasn't right, and we knew it. A nurse emerged abruptly from the door behind us.

"Angie Smith." My stomach jumped.

"We'll be right back, Mom." I looked into the depths of her eyes, and I thought I saw a glimpse of fear.

"Everything will be fine," she said softly.

I kissed her cheek.

"Praying for you, hon." She squeezed my hand, and Todd and I disappeared into the corridors that now hold the worst memories of my life.

The enemy pursues me,
he crushes me to the ground;
he makes me dwell in darkness
like those long dead.
So my spirit grows faint within me;
my heart within me is dismayed.
Psalm 143:3–4

Yet I am always with you;
you hold me by my right hand.
You guide me with your counsel,
and afterward you will take me into glory.
Whom have I in heaven but you?
And earth has nothing I desire besides you.
My flesh and my heart may fail,
but God is the strength of my heart
and my portion forever.
Psalm 73:23–26